FIRST DO NO HARM

Because prophylaxis is better than cure

Farhat Fatima

INDIA • SINGAPORE • MALAYSIA

Copyright © Farhat Fatima 2025
All Rights Reserved.

ISBN

Paperback 979-8-89699-972-0

Hardcase 979-8-89724-951-0

This book has been published with all efforts taken to make the material error-free after the consent of the author. However, the author and the publisher do not assume and hereby disclaim any liability to any party for any loss, damage, or disruption caused by errors or omissions, whether such errors or omissions result from negligence, accident, or any other cause.

While every effort has been made to avoid any mistake or omission, this publication is being sold on the condition and understanding that neither the author nor the publishers or printers would be liable in any manner to any person by reason of any mistake or omission in this publication or for any action taken or omitted to be taken or advice rendered or accepted on the basis of this work. For any defect in printing or binding the publishers will be liable only to replace the defective copy by another copy of this work then available.

CONTENTS

ACKNOWLEDGEMENTS

I would like to begin by thanking the Almighty for His grace, guidance, and strength throughout this journey. Writing this book has been a journey of reflection, growth, and understanding.

I am deeply grateful to everyone who has supported me, particularly to my near and dear ones for their guidance and encouragement. Your wisdom and dedication have inspired me to explore these complex issues with a deeper understanding.

To my parents, whose wisdom and sacrifices have shaped who I am today—thank you for being my constant source of strength.

A heartfelt thanks to all the individuals whose stories, experiences, and wisdom have shaped the pages of this book. Your contributions, big and small, have added depth and color to this narrative.

I'm also grateful to the officials (team) of Notion press for their valuable cooperation.

Lastly, I want to extend my deepest thanks to each and every one of you for taking the time to read my work.

PREFACE

This book is for people (patients) and healthcare professionals; in short, this book is for everyone. 'First do no harm' will take you on a journey through time and love bounded by the responsibility that arises towards society, inspired by real events that have left an indelible mark on my heart and mind.

A doctor just sees the diseases; people see the patient, but only the patient and their loved ones are aware of the struggles and challenges they have faced since years. I have tried to make the reader see behind the scenes, the moments of joy and sorrow, the reality and the journey of life.

As you turn the pages, you will step into the ordinary, relatable story that gives extraordinary lessons. It is my hope that this book will inspire a deeper understanding of the importance of patient safety and the need for systemic reforms in healthcare.

The names of the characters in this book have been changed to protect their privacy and maintain confidentiality.

The information provided in this book is for informational purposes only and is not intended to replace professional medical advice, diagnosis, or treatment. I, the author does not make any representations regarding the accuracy or applicability of the information to individual circumstances.

I have tried my best to explain the medical terminologies in simple words so that no one (from a non-medical background) has to do the efforts that I made in searching these terminologies (in difficult situations to understand the condition of patient).

Note:- A legal warning that any dispute will be done in the Court of Allahabad.

CHAPTER 1

In the book of life, every day adds a new page, written with both laughter and tears, of triumphs and setbacks. Life's journey is never predictable, we learn that it's not just the destination that matters, but the collection of memories, the lessons learned, and the courage to keep moving forward.

School days, coaching, and board results are special for everyone, but the experiences are different. Everyone has some fond memories and stories of the challenges they have faced. My experiences were no different, some problems along with some moments of laughter, from studying seriously to running away from coaching after hearing about a surprise test. In my coaching there was a staircase in front and one at the back side, there were shops on the ground floor.

One day, during a Physics class, the unmistakable aroma of *'Biryani'* wafted up from the ground floor shop diverted the attention of student from the definition of convex and concave lenses, our physics teacher while writing on the board said "Wow! What a nice smell of

Biryani." We all laughed suddenly on listening to this but as soon as he realized that it will disturb the class next to ours, he quickly brought the focus back to studies. In coaching we just try to focus on completing the notes but only self-study is what really matters during exams.

Without marriage parties, births, deaths and someone's illness, the board exams remain incomplete. After the boards, it seems that everyone will become doctors and engineers. On top of that, people ask, "In which college are you taking admission?" This is just a way to start the conversation. Before answering, one gets a long lecture in the form of advice. These people are like a testing machine that tells you in 2 minutes what you can do and what you will not be able to do. After the boards, everyone started filling out the admission forms confidently.

I, an introvert girl, waiting for the results, came to know that the registration process for admission had closed. My mother was also diagnosed with diabetes and kidney related infections. Her urine report showed alarming results—haematuria (presence of blood in the urine) and a culture that revealed *Klebsiella* and *E. coli* infections. I started becoming very worried. People were giving only one piece of advice: "Take her to a good allopathic doctor", they insisted, as if a title could solve everything. "Take her to a good doctor; things won't work without antibiotics." (People were judging the doctors by counting their degrees, a doctor with a lot of degrees is considered to be a good doctor nowadays).

It is not necessary that you get cured from an illness by a doctor with many degrees; rather, a cure is a gift from

God, which He gives to those whose intentions and faith are noble, not on the basis of their degrees and the beauty of the infrastructure of hospital and clinics.

Medicine is a noble profession, not because it treats, but because of the noble intentions of those who treat. Every method of treatment and every invention is based on this spirit.

My mother decided to consult a good homeopathic doctor as allopathic treatment doesn't suit her well. I felt scared, but she told me that in allopathy its treatment is only antibiotic which will damage the kidneys and after sometime that too becomes resistant and once the kidneys get damaged, the last option left will be dialysis or transplantation. Like everybody, I thought that it was her fear, so I researched a lot to clear her doubts, but I ended up discovering that what she is saying is true. She was definitely not a doctor, but she reads about recent research and articles published in magazines and newspapers daily which has enhanced her knowledge a lot about almost every topic, from kitchen tips and recipes to scientific research. So, instead of wasting my time listening to people, I supported her, and she consulted a homeopathic doctor. People laughed at us, and called this our fear. According to them, I was not a good daughter because I was not taking her to an allopathic doctor, so they called me weak and careless.

The doctor gave her medicines, and after taking two doses, her condition worsened. Seeing this, my confidence wavered. But instead of changing the doctor, she informed the doctor about her condition over the phone, and he told her to continue the same medicine for a day or two to get relief and stop only if there was no improvement. Normally, people run away from homeopathic treatment, saying that it will aggravate the disease. Being so worried, I told her to change the doctor, but she continued the medicine for two days, and her condition improved. Was it my mother's faith, her courage, her faith in homeopathy or the fear of allopathy. Only God knows...

She taught me that

- ✦ you know yourself better than anyone else
- ✦ Life is a mix of good and bad; choose wisely, for you alone are responsible for your decisions. (whether you decide from your intuition or from someone's suggestion).

How did she gain this awareness? Why was she so afraid of Western treatment?

To understand this, one will have to go back two decades. It was the year 1989, and my parents' marriage was two months away when my mother had a toothache, for which she consulted a doctor. The doctor gave her medicines and told her to take an additional tablet only if she did not get any relief. My mother took the medicines but did not get relief. When the pain became more severe, she took the other medicine. The pain was relieved, but her urinary tract became blocked. Advice, referral and treatment of several doctors were provided, but the urine problem was not resolved. Her family hospitalised her. A catheter was inserted, medicines were given, and she was discharged after two days. She was unable to stand on her own from the hospital bed. Her family members supported her, thinking she was unable to stand due to weakness.

When she came back home, she could not stand up again. This was not weakness; it was Paraplegia (Paraplegia is paralysis that affects the legs, making it impossible to stand or walk). In this way, the girl, whose marriage preparations were underway, became dependent on a wheelchair. Happiness was overshadowed by sadness. But by the grace of God, my mother's strong willpower, her courage, the support and prayers of family and friends, and after two months of treatment, she was able to stand on her feet again. My mother's family asked my grandparents to cancel the wedding, but instead of canceling the wedding, they postponed it. In this way, my parents' wedding was postponed, and they got married on 14th February.

Her treatment was still going on when my grandfather consulted an experienced and senior doctor in his department who told him that there is no treatment for her condition in medical science right now, from here to abroad, and that she will never be able to become a mother because her nerves have been damaged due to paralysis. If this happens, it will be a miracle of God.

This was shocking news for my family. People gave their opinions on everything from divorce to my father's second marriage. After a lot of prayers, God blessed my parents with a daughter. I was that miracle. Apart from my parents, my grandparents and both my uncles loved me a lot. The wounds of my mother and her family were not yet healed when another incident turned my parents' life upside down.

Due to the delay in the arrival of the doctor and the lack of timely treatment during my mother's second delivery, she lost her second daughter. Along with that, her hope of becoming a mother in future was also lost because, to save her life the doctors had performed a partial hysterectomy (During a partial hysterectomy, a surgeon only removes the upper portion of the uterus). Seeing her critical condition, even after trying a lot, the doctors gave up, but then, suddenly, she regained her breath. In this way, God gave her a second chance of life.

This medical negligence had created a fear of hospitals in my family. Somewhere they had lost faith in the healthcare system. Everyone started trying to forget it by considering it a bad incident, but it was not that easy...

- Is it in the power of a human being to run away from the hospitals, doctors, and treatment?

And now, after so many years, she was still fighting for 'what is right according to others?' and 'what is right for her?' Because in truth, the court is not the only place where evidence is demanded, life itself is a constant trial—a journey where we are asked to prove ourselves not just once, but time and time again.

Amid the chaos of my stagnant life and countless worries, I found myself slipping into depression. I was unable to see any way out; it seemed as if my life had come to an end. My mother's treatment was ongoing when, during a routine visit, the doctor asked me, "What are you doing/studying?" This is a very common and worst question when you are not doing anything? My mother told him that due to my illness and all these stresses, she had not taken admission in college this year. The doctor simply said "Whatever happens, happens for the good." He gave his example, and encouraged me to take admission in college. I got a good rank in a good college but could not take admission. I took admission in another college, left it, and he is saying that whatever happens, happens for the good.

- ✦ Did this bad incident really happened for the good...??
- ✦ Is it true that time gives answers to some questions..?
- ✦ Will my mother's belief prove right or people's words?

CHAPTER 2

As time passed, my mother's health slowly began to improve but her treatment was not even completed when my grandmother suddenly fell ill. My mother became busy taking care of my grandmother and doing household chores.

After 6 months, I took admission for graduation. I got busy with college, theory, practicals, assignments and soon the exams came.

Writing lengthy answers in the exam became the most important task right from the boards. And it becomes more difficult if you have the habit of writing *'to the point'* answers. Every time while writing, one answer would definitely get missed. The tips given by my Zoology professor for getting first division solved my problem. Those tips were:

- ✦ If you are unable to write a lengthy answer, then write in points.
- ✦ Write answers in the form of a flowchart.

- Learn key headings and explain each one in a few lines.
- Use labelled diagrams to explain your topic.
- Make sure to underline scientific names and important points.
- By doing this, all the points will be covered in the answers, the answer will be impressive, and you will get good marks.

It started raining heavily on the first day of my practical. Due to the heavy rain, I met with a minor accident on the way. I somehow managed to reach my college and completed the practical. But that was just the beginning of it. After the rest of the practicals, the preparation for theory exams started. The day before the first theory paper, my grandmother passed away. We were all shattered by her sudden death. I couldn't even think about giving the exam in the morning. But my mother, and my maternal aunts had encouraged me and that's how I gave my graduation first year exams. Then I fell sick, and my father suffered from kidney stone pain. After hearing about my grandmother's death, everyone was coming to meet us. The entire exam period went like this. Whenever an interruption occurs in any work, it comes with such intensity that it feels as if the whole world to be involved in stopping it. The same was happening with my graduation exams.

Still, amidst the chaos, I learned one of the hardest but most essential lessons: Life doesn't pause for your grief. In the end, it was the support of those around me, particularly my mother, that kept me going.

Happiness and sorrow are a part of life, be it sadness, trouble or happiness, everything will pass but memories are left behind either it was good or bad. After some time, I got busy with the preparations and shopping for my cousin's wedding. Suddenly, I got news about the results on the WhatsApp group. Everyone's heartbeat started increasing out of fear, and discussions about the papers began... Paper was very good. The first paper was easy, and hearing this our already elevated BP increased further, "Questions came from the topics which we had skipped."..."There was no time left in the second paper so I missed one answer, because the answers were so lengthy." It gave me some relief to hear that at least there is someone who are like us. When the results came, I was thrilled to see that I had passed with a first division. This felt like a small victory, given everything that had transpired. Of course, I always shared my happiness with my mother, so she hugged me and gave me all her blessings. We were also happy because I had passed my exams in the worst circumstances. My mother reminded me of the incident of the board results.

Oh yes! I remember how I was crying even after getting good marks in the board exams. Everyone thought that I had failed. My uncle came with a box of *Rasgulle (Gulab Jamun*), and everyone told me that instead of being thankful to God, I was crying. Then I got a call from a friend... I told her my result, and she started laughing. She told me that her result was not so good; in one subject, she had failed, but overall she had passed. She said, "Overall,

I have passed. I am eating *Laddu (dessert)*. You also eat *Laddu*! Come on! Celebrate; we have cleared the board exams." Then I started laughing after seeing her positive attitude, and everyone in my home became happy as if it were some festival. Wow! The board results gave me a big lesson in life: ***happiness is not in your achievements; it is a state of mind.***

Back to present-

That's how the second year of college went by, and in the third year, our college came on the list of 'A' grade colleges. May be the last year, which was considered bad for not taking admission, happened for the better...! In this way, I completed my graduation with sweet and bitter memories.

In every person's life there are some prayers which get fulfilled like a miracle as soon as they asked for. Something similar happened to me during PG admission. After admission, the classes started, and as the session was a bit late, preparations for the semester began. As there was not much time left, everyone got busy with practicals, presentations and assignments. A girl like me, who had always been worried about studies, was enjoying her college life and studies this time, even after facing a lot of problems and the credit for this goes to one of my friends who was in the second year of PG, as she guided me very well regarding PG and also helped me by providing notes. The first semester exams were over, and then the second semester started.

In the second semester, I was unable to attend college for 10-12 days due to stomach infection and it seemed that I would not be able to appear for the exams either. However, my teachers and friends helped me a lot in completing my notes. In this way, God gave me so much strength that I attended my exams. Now, it was time for the third semester. This time, four to five days before the mid-term, my aunty, who had been undergoing dialysis at a well-known hospital in Lucknow for the last 1.5 years, slipped into coma. After going through painful treatments such as being in the ICU, on a ventilator, undergoing dialysis and numerous bandages as part of her treatment, she left us all in a few days. Her demise shattered us all.

The night before the exam, I received this heart-wrenching news and I had to leave for Lucknow. When I returned after 4 days, the exam was already over. But there was a sense of satisfaction in my heart, knowing that I hadn't missed my exam, even though I was fully aware that it was already over. When I went to college, everyone was asking me why I missed the exam, and I had no answer. Then, suddenly, a notice came at the college announcing a re-examination. The exam I missed had been cancelled and was rescheduled. This felt like a miracle to me.

- I have learnt two things from this incident.
- First, when we stand up for our loved ones, God stands up for us.
- And second, people say that the past does not come back. But when God comes to support you, He can bring back the time that has already passed.

Surely Allah is most capable of everything (Al-Quran 2:109)

The deficiency remains in our own trust; otherwise, nothing is impossible for Him. If we truly trust God, then our belief has the strength that can change the past in our favor.

CHAPTER 3

The fun of the farewell party amidst the tension of final semester classes, assignments, files and thesis; this is what we call life, a union of sorrow and happiness. The final marksheet of my post-graduation gave me the courage to move ahead. Finally, it felt like life was coming on track.

As children, our dreams are boundless, painted in hues of imagination and wonder, but as we grow up, time changes people, forcing them to compromise with circumstances. My mother was always my strength in difficult situations. Her sacrifices for my education were countless. So my only wish was to achieve something good in my career and give some happiness to my parents.

2019, a new year filled with new hopes. Like every year, this time too, my mother surprised me on my birthday by making my favourite dessert, and she had also cooked my favorite dishes for both lunch and dinner. Although she had been suffering from knee pain for a few days, she forgot everything in the excitement of my birthday. But my father reminded her of doctor (whom my cousin had insisted for), and after a little discussion, he decided to take her to that doctor next day. This was the beginning of 2019, which changed my life as the year went by.

The next day my father took an appointment with the doctor for his consultation. Knee pain has become very common among women in their 50s. People are busy with their lives, using ointments or oils when they feel pain.

But can you imagine where this treatment for her knee pain would lead her?

THE JOURNEY OF ALLOPATHIC TREATMENT WAS STARTED FROM HERE.

It had been only three days since she started taking medicine when she noticed *swelling* in her *ankle*. Now, when my father went and told the doctor about it, the doctor told him to get a KFT test done. After seeing the serum creatinine in the KFT (kidney function test) report, which was near the normal range, he advised him to consult a nephrologist.

Then we took her to a top nephrologist in the city. He wrote down some tests and said that the swelling was not due to the kidneys and advised us to consult an orthopedist (bone specialist). When we went to the bone specialist, an X-ray was done, and he said that there was no fracture and he advised us to consult with a sugar specialist.

Out of worry, my mother went back to homeopathy. But the situation here was like ***'all that glitters is not gold'***.

Those doctors who used to treat serious diseases by giving 2-3 bottles of sweet pills for a reasonable fee, now they are like *Homo sapiens*, who are extinct or may be on the list of highly endangered species. Saving them is of utmost importance, and nobody is paying attention to this.

It has become an emerging trend among homeopathic doctors as well that (in spite of diagnosing diseases by symptoms) they will prescribe some tests before giving medicine, then they give you bottles of tonics in your hands along with expensive medicines.

One week after treatment, what was only swelling earlier has now turned into rashes, an allergy, and small wounds.

Now what?..what now...? People have shown us the fear of cellulitis leading to gangrene and amputation. So, now it's time to consult a sugar specialist. The doctor examined her ankle and explained that he is going to start the treatment, and if he is not able to manage it, he will send her to a nephrologist. I had already consulted a nephrologist, so we have decided to start his treatment.

The wound started healing with the continuous dose of antibiotics from this treatment, which continued for about a month, but the swelling was still there. I used to get worried, thinking about what effect so much treatment would have on someone who was allergic to allopathic medicine. The wound healed, but the swelling remained. In the meantime, she suffered from hypoglycemia (low blood sugar levels) multiple times, and her blood sugar dropped to life-threatening levels.

Meanwhile, someone told my father about a homeopathic doctor. He gave two doses of medicine, and the swelling that my mother had been experiencing for 4-6 months disappeared after just those two doses. Her health also began improving considerably. After so many days, it felt like life was finally returning to normal again. Now, we were feeling the worth of all those blessings which we had taken for granted in life. But after 15 days of treatment, just like the swelling, the doctor also disappeared. When my father went to get the medicine, he came to know that doctor was out of town to attend a wedding. When my father went the next day, he found out that the doctor hadn't come yet. On the third day, he received the same reply, and this disrupted the treatment. Now, after 15-20 days, the antibiotics started showing their side effects. The sugar level (hypoglycemia) that dropped to 30 every morning completely took away my sleep. Serum creatinine also rose to 2.4.

It was once again time to visit a nephrologist. So we consulted a nephrologist at a so-called *'Bada Hospital'*. The doctor had seen all her reports and advised my mother to get admitted. When my mother refused, the doctor prescribed injections and medicines. It was a 5-day treatment. An employee of the hospital standing outside the doctor's room said, "Take it for 3 days, because you will definitely be here by the 4th day." These sentences, said with confidence, sounded a bit strange but were understood after 3 days. Three days of medication, costing us over 3,000 rupees, left my mother in a condition where she needed to be admitted in the hospital. The treatment, which was supposed to be a lifeline, only deepened our fears. It felt as if we were drowning in the very system meant to save us.

I was trying hard just to save her from hospital. But as people say, humans have no control over fate. Managing a person with hypoglycemia at home without medicines was perhaps not possible, but the fear of going to hospital managed to sustain that too for a few days. But listening to people's continuous advice, suggestions, and taunts, has shaken my confidence in my own efforts.

Now it was the turn of another top nephrologist of the city. The scene here was such that the crowd of people was waiting for their turn. Kidney failure patients of all ages were present here. Due to fluid accumulation, there was swelling in some patients' eyes, some had swelling in their legs, and some had swelling in their entire body. After seeing this, I came to understand how swelling in the legs of a kidney patient looks like. This was no less than a scary scene. I took a special number for an urgent visit. This special number cost Rs. 1500/- and it still made us wait for an hour because there was a long queue for special number also.

Here, the doctor prescribed a folley (catheter) to eliminate the infection along with antibiotic injections and medicines. The doctor told us to do the treatment at home by arranging a nurse or at a nearby nursing home, as per your convenience. My mother refused for catheter remembering her bitter experience with it 30 years ago. But the doctor said that it was necessary to eliminate the infection, so he assured her that it would be removed once the infection came under control and told us to visit the next day with ultrasound report. So she agreed after knowing that it's just a matter of few days.

The ultrasound was done the next day, we went to the doctor's clinic, everyone was waiting for their turn. Suddenly, some people arrived in a car, carrying a small child. They all seemed very worried. When I saw the child, his small hands and feet were badly swollen. His cute face had been changed due to the swelling. His big eyes had become smaller due to the swelling, and along with the tears, many questions seemed to float in them. "What was my fault? For what reason did I get punished??" His mother was standing, holding him on her shoulder, so I made her sit and I sat on the stool in front of them. When I asked, "What happened to him?" she told us "My child was fine; he had just a fever and diarrhea. We thought about the best treatment and decided to take him to a good doctor, who admitted him to his hospital (the so-called *'Bada Hospital'*) where, within two days, God knows what treatment was given, that the child's kidneys failed after which they referred us to this doctor."

While saying this, she was crying and saying repeatedly "We had thought of taking him to a good doctor, my child was well, he was playing. Now, he is in this worst condition and is not even talking." While crying, she was blaming herself for taking her son to doctor. Some of the people sitting nearby started criticizing that hospital; they also had their own experiences, I felt that I was the only victim. When I was thinking this, a man, who might have been that child's father or uncle, came with a file in his hand, took out a paper from the file and gave it to the child's mother, saying that the doctor has refused to show this paper. He took the file and moved towards the doctor's cabin. This paper was the prescription for the treatment from that hospital. The way that child's mother told it, led us to conclude from some earlier incidents where treatment became easier after the doctor picked up the wrong medicine given by some other doctor. Suddenly, it came out of my mouth "You must show it to the doctor, this might make the treatment easier." The patient sitting in front also started saying, "Don't forget to show it to the doctor." My number to show the report to doctor had came, so I left... I came back home... But with one fear and one question -

- Are these medicines being given for the disease or
- Are the disease is because of the medicine??

As I reflected on that question, I realized with a chilling certainty that we had all been pawns in a system that seemed to thrive on misdiagnosis, overmedication, and a failure to truly heal. The truth became impossible to ignore. Our faith in the system was crumbling. And with it, I could feel my own hope slipping away.

Would we ever find the right treatment? Or were we doomed to repeat this cycle of suffering and uncertainty?

CHAPTER 4

My mother's blood glucose levels began to fall repeatedly, raising the question of where she should be admitted for treatment. For me, it was a constant battle, not just with my mother's fluctuating blood sugar levels, but also with an overwhelming system that seemed to offer more obstacles than solutions. It was decided that if she had to be admitted to a hospital, why not admit her to the hospital in my father's office department? This would make it easier to refer her to a good hospital in the Delhi region, if required, as per the facility my father was entitled to.

She headed to the hospital with us, without anyone's help. It was only then that I realized how much I had unknowingly managed her hypoglycemia. But despite her sugar levels being within range, the doctor, alarmed by the sudden drop earlier, decided to keep her in the ICU for closer monitoring. Everyone is aware of the conditions of government hospitals. The ICU was just like the general ward of any private hospital or perhaps even worse than that.

The treatment started like this: a nurse did the sugar test and said, "It is normal, why was she kept in ICU?". God knows what strength He gave me; it was difficult for me to even understand how things were managed. Well, I told them that I had given her honey and sugar at home and it became normal, but after a few hours or maybe by the next day, it would go down again." It was clear that her condition needed more than just quick fixes.

To start the treatment, she first took the sample, and in the meantime, instructed the other nurse to insert a catheter. I rushed away to ask the doctor something, but I couldn't bear the thought of leaving her alone, so I ran back as quickly as I could. When I returned, I heard her screams, and I ran towards her. But they stopped me, saying that the nurse was inserting catheter and vigo (IV cannula). I knew her level of patience, so I didn't believe it. When I went inside after taking permission, I saw that even after hurting the patient so much and despite her efforts, she hadn't been able to insert the catheter. She left it and started inserting the IV cannula (Vigo). She inserted the needle once, but there was no blood. Then she inserted it again and again. In this manner, she repeatedly inserted the needle from the wrist to the elbow, pulling it out each time. She kept saying that God knows where the vein is, as she was unable to find it properly.

This was the condition of ICU nursing staff, looking as if she was experimenting on the patient. I requested her to call the other nurse (who had taken the sample) and let her try. The nurse angrily told me that go and call her on your own, we were shocked when we heard this, then another woman, who had been quietly assisting the nurse, made a quick call to the head nurse, requesting her assistance in inserting catheter and vigo. The head nurse inserted the needle and the vigo was fixed easily in just one attempt. After trying a couple of times the catheter was also inserted and not a single scream came out.

A hospital is probably such a place where you do not know how much pain is a part of your treatment, and how much extra you are receiving that you do not deserve.

It was time for the doctor's rounds, so the doctor came. My mother was on the first bed, the head nurse while giving the file to the doctor, asked us - "Has she undergone any surgery earlier"??

"Yes," my father said. "About 24 or 25 years ago…" then he recounted the medical history, which stretched back over two decades.

The nurse said to the doctor "The surgery hadn't been performed correctly Sir, the surgery had caused an obstruction in the bladder". Suddenly, it came out of my mouth, "Can this be treated?" The answer I got was "Yes".

This is not just "Yes", but a long-awaited answer to a problem that had gone undiagnosed for 25 years. It was like a ray of hope for a person who had been sitting in darkness for decades hoping for light. When the wait is as long as ours, hopes are broken and even prayers that have been accepted become hard to believe. I told this to my mother and then decided to take opinion of another doctor who also advised us for some test to diagnose clearly whether the treatment is possible or not. But a person who is tired of undergoing test after test without any relief often gives up one step before success. Now things were clear to a great extent. The doctor once again told us about the same test and treatment.

Now we just had to wait for the infection to subside and for the symptoms to improve. I went back to the hospital and informed my mother. The infection was eliminated through the catheter in 2 to 3 days, but the course of antibiotics has to be completed. She was shifted from ICU to HDU on the first day itself. The cleaning staff lady in both ICU and HDU was sitting there eating *'Paan' (betel leaves)* and ordering the patient's attendant to do the patient's work on their own. Every time a new medicine was prescribed for the pain caused by other medicines. In this way, apart from the injections and medicines prescribed by the nephrologist, God knows how many other medicines and injections were given.

Only one person was allowed to stay with the patient, so my mother told me to go home. During this hospital stay, I came back home after midnight daily with my uncle, and my father stayed at the hospital.

After five days, the doctor told us to go and consult with the nephrologist for further treatment. I went with my uncle, and as soon as I reached there, I saw that the nephrologist, along with his family was going out of town. His driver moved the car, but when the doctor saw me, he told his driver to stop the car. He then asked me whether I had consulted earlier. I said, "Yes, my mother is admitted in the hospital." He took the file, checked the reports, and prescribed injections and medicines for further treatment while sitting in the car. I thanked him and wished them for a happy journey. It was just a few seconds and a doctor's concern that saved us.

In these 8-9 days, I have seen a lot of things, such as different types of patients, their conditions and problems. A cancer patient, his family, parents, sisters, young wife and 6-month-old daughter who were witnessing the last days of his life.

The struggle of a family caring for a loved one paralyzed for five long years, a journey filled with unspoken pain, quiet resilience, and the weight of unyielding hope. The challenges faced by the patients and their families who have come from far away for treatment.

Meanwhile, on Bed Number 1, a patient was admitted in HDU, in a very critical condition, but after a few hours, the patient went missing, and the whole staff got busy in searching for him. The staff was in a panic when the patient was not found on the bed. Where did he go?

The Doctor's rounds were going on and on bed no. 9, an old aged patient who started using the spirometer (respirometer) to exercise as soon as he saw the doctor, and the doctor laughed and scolded him, saying..."I know, you started exercising with the respirometer as soon as you saw me". Upon hearing this, the patient started juggling three balls with full energy. An elderly man came to his bed and both were surprised to see each other and recognized each other, both started remembering the old office days. Looking at both of them, it seemed as if they were not suffering from any disease. That old patient was looking absolutely fine and his friend... he was the same lost patient from bed no. 1 who had been admitted in critical condition to the HDU some time ago, and now the entire staff was searching for him. Does friendship really has the power to make hard time easier? Everyone there was witnessing the answer.

My attention was diverted when my mother waved her hand, and the bottle hanging on the saline stand turned. The bottle seemed different so I checked the name... *Metronidazole*... who prescribed this? We immediately ran to the senior nurse (nursing in charge) and told her, "The patient is allergic to metrogyl. The doctor has already been informed about this. Then who prescribed it?" Upon hearing this, the nurse who had administered it, ran towards my mother and quickly changed the bottle and started withdrawing the medicine from the syringe, when blood started coming out, she connected it to the other bottle and she left. This mistake occurred because she had earplugs in and was distracted by her mobile. As a result, she gave my mother's medication to the other patient and vice versa, leading to unnecessary harm to patients and the doctor being held accountable for the mistake that he had not done. This was HDU, where they paid attention when I complained, but in the general ward, they didn't even bother to remove the earplugs before 15 minutes.

The pain and humiliation of the hospital now started to flow in the form of tears, but the attendant tolerates everything for the sake of the patient. The outcome of a patient's treatment, I realized, depends not only on medical expertise but also on the compassion, diligence, and integrity of the people who deliver it. Without that, even the best treatments may fall short.

The cleaning staff was not doing their duty, the nurse giving extra pain to the patient, dealing with all this and saving the patient from the negligence of the general ward, requesting to shift the patient to HDU after contacting people despite the genuine reason of the patient's blood glucose level being low, the behaviour of the HDU staff and the taunts of the doctor, who said, "Go and consult senior doctor", and when we did the same, he told us that "What the senior nephrologist has done, he just prescribed the antibiotics. Her kidneys will fail very soon, now prepare for dialysis". Such sentences were uttered in front of the patient. Instead of showing hope they were showing despair or may be the truth of today's society, because it was bitter to hear. It happens, but at least he had a chance to show his capabilities. It was better than blaming others. The deaths of patients was revealing this defeat. When the doctor told duty doctor for discharge, we got her discharged on the same day and took her home. With the prayer that we would never have to see the hospital again. But we were unaware that the journey written in our destiny was yet to come.

I came to know from here that not only doctors, but also their helping hands, are playing a vital role in medical negligence.

- ✦ What effects do these issues have on the outcomes of treatment??

CHAPTER 5

The medicines I received after discharge from the hospital was three times the number of medicines prescribed by the nephrologist. "Where will the person go after taking so many medicine? Why have they given too many medicines? Even the doctor has not prescribed this." The reply I got was "Don't try to become a doctor. Give her properly whatever has been prescribed. He is a doctor; he knows more than you." This sentence is the full stop of the conversation.

One of the biggest challenges for diabetic patients in the hospital is the insulin injection. Administering it to someone already on medication can render those very medicines ineffective, creating a complex web of risks.

As the mystery of her disease was resolved halfway, now we were just waiting for the right treatment to be done. From attending the guests who came to see her to making food and from doctor's appointments to tests and medicines I was taking care of my mother and God knows, how I was doing all this and from which strength?

Only a week had passed and suddenly my mother's condition took a terrifying turn. She began to suffer from melena—(melena is caused by bleeding higher up in gastrointestinal GI tract). I decided not to give her another dose as the medicine she had been prescribed contained a blood thinner and I couldn't ignore the possibility that it could worsen the bleeding. But my aunt thought that I was scared, so she took all medicines from my hand and given it to my mother. As the evening wore on, my mother's condition grew worse. Then my aunt sent us to consult her cousin for the right advice. The professor at the medical college, the HOD, and an experienced doctor (within the limits of his specialization, agreed that only he could give the right advice). He showed my mother's reports and treatment records to his student/medical intern, he asked for the diagnosis, asked for treatment, corrected it wherever required and then adviced us to take her to a urologist and gastroenterologist and even suggested for blood transfusion if needed.

Now, from there, I went straight to the urologist. After writing all the tests, he said, "I will do the treatment. Admit her here, and take her to a gastro doctor." After seeing the medicine that we got after hospital discharge, he said that the patient was being given blood thinners and told us to stop this medicine right away. The gastro doctor also had the same reaction; he told us the same thing.

The Gastro doctor had seen the reports and the prescriptions of treatment done so far and told us that it might be the side effects of antibiotics. "Now I'm giving medicines, in case she wouldn't get any relief then a banding procedure may be required." "What is this?" Before asking, he told about Endoscopic Variceal Ligation/ EVL in very simple words which although I heard it, but it went over my head.

Although the gastrointestinal bleeding reduced due to *Trenaxa* but vomiting and weakness deteriorated her condition. The crowd of people made her already bad condition worse. My mother began asking us, "Why are there so many people standing here? Am I going to die?" People had even prepared to recite the *Kalma*. And they started advising us to have patience. I felt completely broken. In this crowd too, there was no one who could listen or understand. My uncle told me, "Don't worry, nothing will happen to her. We will take her to the best hospital." I was shattered and broken, unable to hold back the tears that blurred my vision. I cried out to him, "Please, save her! I can't bear the thought of her going towards dialysis. Please, don't let her suffer like this." My cousin promised me that he would donate blood to my mother if she needed a blood transfusion. My uncle reassured me, "Don't worry, nothing will happen to her. We will admit her to the hospital, shift her to a good hospital in Delhi by tomorrow and get her treated there. She will be fine."

We once again admitted her to the hospital, and in the ICU all the hospital welcome rituals started again. This time again the same nurse who was unable to insert the catheter last time, did it again, when my eyes fell on the urobag, I shouted, as the urobag was completely filled with blood. The nurse quickly called the doctor and showed him the urobag, the doctor said "You have caused an internal injury, put the *Trenaxa* bottle immediately." Her mistake was compensated by my uncle's 1 unit of blood.

A patient who was already on the verge of needing a transfusion due to blood loss. Her negligence had led to more blood loss. But who cares! Orders have been issued to shift the patient only after the blood transfusion.

I spent the entire night crying in the ICU, she also did not slept the entire night and even in the darkness, I didn't know how she understood that I was crying. The night stretched endlessly, each second heavier than the last.

Next day, when it came to the blood transfusion, my cousin who had promised to donate blood, went to the blood bank, but as a man has no control over everything, his blood pressure was high, due to which he did not get permission to donate blood and in the end my uncle donated the blood.

After the blood transfusion, we were trying to get a referral letter when my father said that he wanted to admit her to a hospital in another city whose name I had heard from him since my childhood. Every time the matter of treatment ended with the name of that same hospital. After a lot of discussion, we decided to get her referred to a good hospital in Delhi. As the journey was long, so for patient's convenience, an ICU ambulance in which doctor was also there was booked by paying Rs. 25,000.

My mother reminded me of all the little essentials for the journey that she always kept in her bag during travels like *safety pins, thread and needle, nail cutter, small scissors, soap shampoo,* and some essential medicines, if it was cold weather then a small packet of *cloves, cardamom and mace.* All these things take up less space but are very useful. In spite of so much weakness, it was her willpower which did not let her become weak.

I went back home to pack the bags, my father stayed at the hospital and my uncle went to get the referral papers. After some time, my father called me and informed me that the papers for the hospital in Delhi were ready, get the packing done, we will leave in a few hours. I became anxious and made *'Sadqa'* (Apart from infinite benefits, it is also given to get blessings of the creator to have favorable outcome in different areas such as improvement in health etc.). I prayed to God that she should go wherever it is better for her. Then, I thought, why I'm praying this now when the decision had already been made, the paper work is already done. I just wanted the best treatment, that is why over Lucknow, Kanpur and Delhi I gave preference to Delhi. I should be happy, then why I'm feeling anxious?

I was thinking about this when I got a call from my uncle and he told me that the papers for the hospital my father wanted, have been made.. What is this? A moment ago, my father told me that the papers for the hospital in Delhi were ready. My uncle continued "Yes, I was getting the referral done for Delhi but suddenly a thought struck my mind that we didn't know how many days it would take, Delhi is far away than this city, we too wouldn't be able to reach there soon, no one will be there, how will you manage everything alone, this city is closer, so I requested them to change the name of the hospital." Sadqa and prayers have that power which often changes a decision already taken. Something bad might have been going to happen, but it got postponed due to sadqa. We left for the new city in the morning for her treatment.

CHAPTER 6

Turning point of my life-

As soon as we reached the hospital, we encountered the death of a dialysis patient. We were busy with the formalities of admitting my mother when I saw a lady who was sitting alone on the ground and crying badly, and no one was there to console her. People were passing by as if they had eyes but they could not see anything. I thought I should go and ask the reason why she was crying, but when I saw people ignoring her like this, I didn't get the courage to move forward. I took the papers and moved ahead from the reception towards the emergency. When did my mother teach me to move ahead despite seeing someone in pain?

I entered the emergency ward but turned around and came back, I asked her the reason for crying, then while crying she told me that her mother-in-law had been undergoing dialysis for the past 1.5-2 years. When her condition worsened, we admitted her and now she had died. Upon hearing this, I remembered the same case of my aunt and tears came to my eyes. I had no words to console her, so I passed her the water bottle. Meanwhile, her husband came there. The pain of losing his mother was clearly visible on his face. My father was standing nearby; he gave water to her husband. That lady's *sindoor* in the parting of her hair and a *dupatta* on my head, my father wearing a *kurta-pyjama* and on the other side there was a man with a *Tilak* on his forehead. People standing nearby were looking at us with great surprise; I don't know why. A lady asked me "Who is she?" "I don't know her; I'm new to this city." I replied. Hearing this, she also stopped and the people nearby also came there. Then I told that lady to call someone, and she informed her relatives. "Help someone that much, that they can help themselves further." As soon as I remembered these words of my mother, I moved towards my mother.

In the emergency, the doctor discussed my mother's case history and looking at her condition at that time shifted her to the ICU because she had been transferred here from the ICU. This was the ICU of a private hospital where the meeting time with the patient was limited to just a few minutes in the morning and evening throughout the 24 hours. The topic came up about the *Central line*.

(Central line (or central venous catheter) which is like an intravenous (IV) line —a procedure where a catheter is inserted into a vein near the heart after making an incision, typically used for administering fluids and medication). It might have been made for someone's benefit, but today it is being misused commonly. And who is getting the benefits from it? I came to know about this later... I requested the doctor that when medicine is going through the vigo (IV cannula), then what is the need for central line? With great difficulty, I managed to saved her from the central line. She was saved from cutting the neck (which they call an small incision) and getting a catheter inserted. At that time, it felt like a victory—small, yet meaningful, but a fear was always there. "Will we be able to save ourselves from this evil, spread in the name of treatment? For how long?"

This was the first time when I was unable to meet her, despite being so close to her. I was standing at the door of the ICU. The guard was opening the door only for the staff. After some time, we were called inside asking who is with the patient? My father and I went inside. "Please receive the patient's belongings." I received her bangles, earrings and her clothes which was replaced by a hospital uniform. Meanwhile, the nurse came and said "The nose pin is not being removed, you please take it off." I went near her, she didn't allowed us to remove the nose pin. I asked what difference would this small pin make. The answer I got was that there are many staff members here, and for patient's safety, they hand over the gold and jewellery to patient's attendents. The doctor on duty told us to tell the case history of patient, and then we were sent away with the message that they would call us when doctor comes on his rounds.

When the doctor came, I narrated the entire case history again and also told him what the doctors in my town had said regarding the treatment. "No, this condition will never be cured; she will remain on a catheter throughout her life. There is no treatment for this." These were the words of Dr. Mohit, who did not consider that speaking with such a rude attitude in front of a patient in the ICU might hurt her. After trying unsuccessfully to explain one more time, I kept quiet.

I came out of the ICU and sat on the chair. My aunt had given me the breakfast that she had brought with her while coming to the hospital, I ate a little on her insistence, drank some water and sat there until they called us again. The doctor was on rounds. When I went inside, a senior doctor was standing with Dr. Mohit. "The patient's condition is good, urine output is normal and so are the vitals. I have checked her kidney reports; when the urologist will come, he will tell you the treatment. After keeping her under observation for 24 hours, tomorrow she will be shifted from ICU to ward." After hearing this from a senior doctor I took a sigh of relief. Later, we came to know that this nephrologist was the director of the hospital's nephrology department.

Dr. Mohit was assisting the urologist also. The rounds of both doctors took place in Dr. Mohit's presence. Dr. Mohit said to the urologist, who was looking at the patient's file, "She is saying that treatment for her condition is possible; the patient may recover". "Yes, she is right, if her problem is *surgical* and not *neurological*, then the patient may recover". Finally, the urologist (Dr. Ayush) gave hope on which the whole treatment depended. Before I could feel happiness, I realized that the words of the urologist had hurt Dr. Mohit's ego. My happiness was overshadowed by fear. The urologist continued that what would be the treatment if it was a neurological problem and what would be the treatment if it was due to wrong surgery, but to reach any conclusion, a test would have to be done.

This was the same test that was advised in Allahabad. The urologist said that we will get the test done by today or tomorrow. "Let it be for now, she will be discharged in 2-3 days and when she becomes a little stable, get it done after three weeks or 20 days." Dr. Mohit interrupted in between... The Urologist agreed with what the doctor said "It's okay, then give her a date after 20 days." I tried to tell him but he stucked to his words. After waiting for 25 years, the unnecessary wait of 20 days felt like 20 years... The Doctor postponed the test; anyone could easily feel the negative vibes that his ego got hurt, but can we discuss (argue) with the doctor while standing in the ICU?

- A doctor's ego—can it really hurt a patient?
- Western medicine, with all its advancements, has shifted the focus of human thinking from *'treatment'* and *'cure'* to *'management'* and *'transplant'.*

CHAPTER 7

After 24 hours, she was shifted from the ICU to a private ward. Doctor told us that she is in stable condition now and that they will discharge her the next day. While discussing the treatment, they learned about her recent blood loss and gastrointestinal problem (although I had already informed them while writing the case history in the ICU, whether they missed it or the doctor had ignored this while reading). After hearing this, the senior nephrologist (Dr. Abhay) standing there told them to send the patient for an upper GI Endoscopy. Dr.Mohit interrupted him by saying that refer the patient for lower GI Endoscopy, but his senior referred her to the Gastro unit for UGI Endoscopy as per her symptoms. When she was going for Endoscopy in the ambulance, the hospital staff stopped us, saying that only one person is allowed to go with the patient. After requesting them they allowed us to go with her.

Nurse took her inside for Endoscopy and they told us to wait outside on chairs. I was scared hearing the screams of patients coming from the Endoscopy room. After about 40 to 45 minutes, the nurse came and told me to go inside.

When I went inside my legs were trembling... what would I get to hear now?? When I went near her, I saw tears streaming down her face and I had no words to console her.

The doctor had an endoscope in his hand and some images of food pipe *(esophagus)* were flashing on the screens in front, which were completely beyond my understanding. The doctor asked me, "Had she suffered from Jaundice earlier?" "No, not yet, but 25 years ago and was cured after treatment." I replied. Then he said, "Her liver is damaged." Listening to this, I felt as if the ground had slipped beneath my feet. I felt this on the fifth floor of that building. "But we had brought her here for kidney treatment." Saying this, I took two steps back in a state of shock and got hit by her stretcher and when I saw the tears flowing from her eyes, I came out from there.

As soon as I came out of the endoscopy room, I lost my patience and started crying. My father and aunt started asking me what happened? What did the doctor said? The doctor is saying that her liver is damaged. I had brought her here for kidney treatment. How far has the treatment of knee pain taken us.

The nursing staff who accompanied her from the hospital informed us that we will have to wait for some time to collect the reports, as instead of one, two additional procedures had been done. "But we were informed about the endoscopy only." "Yes, but three tests/ procedures were done."

After getting the reports, we came back to the hospital. What extra procedures was done? How it was done? Why was it done? I couldn't know anything… Dr.Mohit came, and as usual, taunted us and went towards the general ward. This time, when the nurse saw me crying, she said, "He shouts like this at everyone… this is how he takes out his frustration on us too." My mother was unable to say anything because of pain that she had just gone through. The pain she got in the name of the test was clearly visible on her face. I went out of the room and sat near the huge glass window near the stairs and sent the reports to her doctor at Allahabad on *WhatsApp* and waited for his reply. Tears were rolling down from my eyes continuously.

Another patient from my city was admitted there, her sister and son narrated her story like this- "She was at home when she suffered from a fever, for which she went to the doctor. The doctor advised for blood test and prescribed medicines for malaria. After taking medicines for 2-3 days her condition deteriorated. When we took her to another doctor, he said that her kidneys had failed, she would have to undergo dialysis and there is no other option. When I (her son) asked him for taking her to Delhi, the doctor said that she is not in condition to go to Delhi. She may die on the way. Somehow, we managed to take her here. Later, it was found out that she hadn't suffered from malaria and she was treated with wrong medication. And that treatment badly affected her *kidneys* and *liver*. She is much better now, and the doctors are discharging her tomorrow." They tried to console me by saying this. Everyone there was trying to console me by giving examples like this. But people themselves forgot to understand that, even here, the critical condition of patient was not because of disease but because of the wrong treatment.

The nurse came and told me that my mother is calling me. I did not want to cry in front of her, that's why I was sitting outside. But how could I hide my tears from my mother? Even my efforts to keep myself normal went in vain. As soon as I went near her, she said to me, "I know why you are sitting outside, why are you crying? You know the doctor told me that my liver has been damaged. Now whatever is meant to happen, will happen." I tried to convince her, "No, the doctor has not seen that report yet… everything will be fine, don't worry." I could feel that her strong willpower had been broken by the words of that doctor. A fear sat deep in my mind, whether treatment of the disease is possible or not, but if she loose her willpower, then nothing will be possible.

There was a South Indian nurse named 'Soni' who was perfect in her nursing work and honest too. She had perfectly inserted the *cannula* every time and kept my mother away from the *central line*. And always performed her duty with complete care.

When the doctor came for rounds, the matter of giving reference to a gastroenterologist for the liver problem came up. My father had heard about two doctors from our relatives, Dr.Mayur and Dr.Ahsan. Regarding Dr. Mayur, it was said that he is a surgeon and my mother needs the treatment of the gastro doctor, so my father asked them about Dr. Ahsan. Upon hearing this, Dr. Mohit said, "Why do you want to consult Dr. Ahsan only." His negative words was clearly pointing to the direction that he was comparing the doctor's name and my father's appearance (his *kurta-pyjama*). I was shocked to hear these words from a person belonging to such a noble profession.

When blood is needed to save a life, the blood group is considered, not the religion..Why? Probably because **the first step of every religion is humanity.**

I said to senior nephrologist, "Sir, we are not from this city, and we don't know any doctors here. My father heard about him from local relatives, that is why he suggested his name. You may call whoever is best in your view. I just want the best treatment for my mother." But the senior nephrologist directed his on-duty staff to refer the case for consultation to the doctor as desired by the patient's attendant. After some time, the nurse informed us that the gastroenterologist would come tomorrow.

On the next day since morning many relatives came there to see my mother. Dr. Ahsan suddenly came into the room and stood near her bed. I asked my aunt about him because I was seeing many relatives for the first time, and a nurse used to come with the doctor, carrying the patient's file, so I got confused. My aunt said, "I don't know him." I went out of the room to call my father and saw the nurse picking up pages of the file from the ground and running towards the room. Then, I understood that he is the gastro doctor who was referred yesterday.

The gastroenterologist had seen the patient's file and started telling my uncle about my mother's illness. I was afraid that if, like the other doctors, he too said something negative in front of my mother, her will power would break completely and then no medicine would be effective. As soon as this thought came to my mind, I quietly told my uncle not to discuss it in front of her. On hearing this, Dr. Ahsan shouted angrily at me: "Why? Why shouldn't we talk in front of her? The patient should be made aware of her condition." We also believe the same and my mother used to see her reports by herself, but from the recent incident, I was scared and stopped them from discussing it in front of her. The gastro doctor left my uncle and turned towards my mother and started talking to her. "You have a liver disease... there is no treatment for it, but it can be controlled with medicines and a good diet. Take high protein diet and your medicines on time and you will be absolutely fine."

After seeing the patient, he went towards the reception and started writing in the file, then my cousin who came from Lucknow to see her went ahead and started discussing the case with him. He told me that the doctor is still here, if you have any queries about diet or treatment ask him... but only one question came out of my mouth, "How her liver got damaged?" He asked, "Did she ever suffered from Jaundice?" "No, not yet. 24-25 years ago at the time of delivery, she suffered from jaundice, but she was treated until the reports came back normal then the doctor stopped the treatment." I replied. Dr.Ahsan then said, "This disease does not occur overnight, it progresses slowly over 10-15 years." But the tests were done regularly, and nothing came out. There were a lot of questions in my mind, it was a shock to get the confirmation of liver damage, and I was unable to ask anything...So he himself started explaining to me that "This disease does not appear in the test, often it gets detected in the end. The patient's life expectancy was only two years, one positive point in her case is that there is no *accumulated fluid* in the liver yet (there is no *ascites*). With good diet and treatment the disease remains under control." He was continuously saying such things as if the questions were written on my face, may be because he deals with same situation every day—a crowd of such patients with a list of the same questions.

The doctor left from there and when I came back, my mother said, "You definitely got scolded but I got to know about my disease. Although my liver is being damaged but with good diet and treatment I will be fine." How easily he explained negative things in a positive way to the patient and left. My mother's broken willpower started getting strengthened along with my courage, which is the first and the strongest part of patient's recovery.

- In that moment, I realized something profound: The words of a doctor can make or break a patient's will to fight. It is the duty of a doctor to tell the patient about their illness, to tell the truth, not to deceive and not to sugar-coat things. But not in such a way that would break the will power of patient because what is not possible for medical science is possible for the Almighty.
- Education is the name of developing critical thinking skills...
- Is that education correct which puts a full stop on the thinking abilities of a person?? Makes it limited??

CHAPTER 8

My father was going to retire from his government job the next day. We had planned many things, such as giving gifts to his office staff and arranging a small celebration. But we were unaware that at that time we would be in a hospital in an unfamiliar new city. His farewell pictures were sent on *WhatsApp* by my younger cousins and my father's colleagues and I showed it to my mother. It was an emotional moment for my father and all of us that a person who had spent a major part of his life in a place, was now going to retire from there. Every morning my mother used to wake up early to prepare tiffin for him and to serve breakfast to everyone in the family, my father used to go to the office and then we wait for him to return home.

It has become common to hear this near retirement: "Now retirement is near, when we will be free, we will sit together and talk freely, planning for going out after retirement. One should never wait for the moment of happiness in life, because sorrow comes without invitation and too much planning ruins the moment of happiness.

I learnt this lesson some time ago. This quotation had changed my thinking a lot... ***"Don't wait for the perfect moment, take the moment & make it perfect".***

Here, the nephrologist had prescribed a high protein diet as per the kidney requirement and advised for blood transfusion. Somehow blood was arranged for transfusion and in the evening one unit of blood transfusion started. My uncle came there and it took the whole day for arranging blood, so I told him to take rest on the side bench and I sat near my mother. There was itching around my mother's hand, when I complained about it to nurse, she said that it happens during blood transfusion, don't worry she will be fine.

Meanwhile, my father came from Allahabad, and he was looking very tired with unhappy moment of such retirement having a deep shock feeling in the painful circumstances. He has come to know that half unit blood had been transfused and there was about two hours remained left for it to be finished.

It was late, around midnight, I was sitting there and looking at each drop of blood. Nurse was coming there from time to time and she told me to sleep and said with a smile "It's my duty, I am here, looking after her, don't worry."

When one is right and other is wrong then whom to trust? I remained awake and when only a small amount of blood left to be transfused, I slept just for 10 minutes and suddenly I got up and saw the nurse was standing beside my mother's bed, she smiled and said, "I am here, don't worry. This is my duty." I felt very good to see how responsible and caring nurse she was.

If every person understands the importance of their duty and responsibility like this, then no one will have to help anyone. Nowadays, we humans have forgotten our responsibility and duty and are busy in helping others by feeling pity for them, without thinking that if we concentrate on our duty then we automatically will help ourselves as well as others.

In the morning, when doctor was on his round, she still had problem of itching in her hand, so the doctor prescribed medicine. There was no relief in the itching even with medicine and rashes also appeared in the body. When the nephrologist had seen her trouble, he prescribed a medicine but the nurse told him that it was not available in their pharmacy, on which the doctor said that it is necessary to have this essential medicine in the pharmacy, so many patients who get blood transfusion here every day would have to face such problem. One patient's suffering had became the catalyst for a change that might help others down the line.

The doctor changed many medicines for her condition, prescribed oil and creams but she did not get any relief, also the pain she was having in her mouth since the time of endoscopy was being treated as a different thing and hence medicines were being prescribed. Due to that pain she was not able to eat anything.

The nephrologist told us that on the suggestion of Dr. Mohit we have decided to shift her to the gastroenterology department and we will tell them to sent her here before discharge for kidney treatment. And he advised Colonoscopy for whose preparation the nurse given us a bottle of *'Colo Prep'* (a bitter solution which was given over night before Colonoscopy) and told us to give it to patient from 12 am as the patient had to be sent for test at 10 am. My mother didn't eat anything after 9 pm. Since the morning at 10:30 am, the staff repeatedly said to wait a little and this continued till 2:30 pm. The patient (my mother) waited for the test without eating for 16-17 hours, then the nurse came and told us that the test is postponed for the next day. She ate very little in the evening. At 12 in the night, again the same *'Colo Prep'* was given and we kept waiting again from next day morning, then at 4:30 in the evening she was shifted to another branch of the hospital where, on complaining to the doctor that the patient's health was deteriorating due to fasting since two days in the name of Colonoscopy, then the doctor told the nurse and sent the patient for Colonoscopy, we got the report. At the time of discharge after a week, it was found out that it was not a *Colonoscopy* but a *Sigmoidoscopy*. After having a wait of two days without eating, some other test was done instead of the test that was recommended. Was this a necessity or a formality or a professional (business) matter?? God knows.

Next day, Dr. Mehra (another gastroenterologist) stopped many medicines. After coming to know about her skin problem, Dr. Mehra gave reference to dermatologist Dr. Priti. The dermatologist prescribed medicines. But neither her allergy (itching) nor the problem in her mouth gotten relief. Dr. Mehra and Dr. Ahsan gave references to different doctors in between. In which the first reference was given to Dr. Mohit for kidney treatment. Both the doctors asked the nurse to call him during their rounds in the morning and evening but he didn't came. We all are aware that excessive use of antibiotics and medicines have a bad effect on the liver. Without providing proper treatment, the antibiotics given continuously were making her liver condition worst and that is why both the gastro doctors were referring to Dr. Mohit on their rounds every day.

It was *Dussehra*, around 4-5 in the evening Dr. Mohit came there and as usual his conversation had started with taunting. "What happened, you are fine here, what is the problem, I got a call from Dr. Ahsan." Looking as if he was waiting for this call. Nurse asked him about further treatment which was getting delayed since 2-3 days because he didn't came. He then looked at the patient's file and again prescribed antibiotic injections and left. Later, the nurse came and said, "I was there in the nephrology department for about 4-6 month, he has a same rude behaviour everyday." She continued, "He was being called since the last 3-4 days, he came today when Sir (Dr.Ahsan) himself called him in the morning and requested to come and see the patient."

At night, when the nurse was giving her medicine and injection through drip, suddenly another nurse came into the room and told the nurse that the condition of the patient in the adjacent room has deteriorated, check him first. My mother sent the nurse away saying, "I'm fine, you should go there as there may be some emergency." The nurse attached the drip and left. Patient's family members were standing outside the room. Seeing the critical condition of the patient he was shifted to the ICU. Later the nurse came and detached the drip and said that it took more time because the patient was shifted to the ICU. Later we came to know that the patient was the uncle of a urologist (Dr. Abhijeet) in the same hospital.

When Dr. Mohit ignored the tests again, next day doctor gave reference to a neurologist for his opinion. For skin rashes she was sent to another dermatologist, and on the advice of the urologist she was sent for USG. So many diseases she got in the treatment of one disease.

My mother narrated the incident of endoscopy that the clamp was put on the mouth in such a way that her tongue got injured and one of the weak teeth got shaken, when she tried to tell, the nurse, thinking it to be the fear of endoscopy held her hand and feet. The injury that remained in the mouth for 15 days, for which many medicines and ointments were prescribed and now she had been irritated even with the treatment.

Somewhere the doctor was also aware of these things. Then on telling about the injury, Dr. Ahsan, after realizing the mistake done in endoscopy, told us that for this problem consultation of dentist is needed. And when he was about to write in the file my mother got angry and scolded him saying "I don't need any treatment now, don't give reference to anyone", he smiled and closed the file.

In this way, every doctor used to comfortably rectify the negligence in treatment by giving reference to another doctor, which was compensated by the patient's bills and the troubles they had to go through.

Meanwhile, one day my mother's condition suddenly deteriorated. Around 11-12 at night she pulled out the cannula from her hand and she started insisting to stop the treatment. Seeing her condition, my father called the nurse. The nurse told him that she is coming in just ten minutes and sent him back. There was neither any doctor nor anyone to attend to the patient. The nurse came and she called the doctor on duty of emergency ward on our insistence. As soon as the doctor came, he asked the nurse to take a blood sample and insert a central line. Again the same topic *'Central Line'*. What is the reason of this condition? Without thinking as to what should be her treatment, the first thing that comes to their minds is central line and to shift the patient to ICU. (As per their protocol). The nurse fixed the vigo (cannula) and took a blood sample, then the nurse herself increased the dosage of a medicine and asked to give it every hour, and said "We see such patients everyday, so don't worry, this medicine will give relief." Holding the hand of my mother in which the nurse had fixed the vigo, I sat beside her. My uncle was coming the next day, on hearing about her condition he left for here, the same night. When I talked to him, he told me that he boarded on the first train that he saw arriving here. Everyone was sleeping at night and he did not know anything about which train it was and when it would arrive. I picked up my mobile and checked the current running status of the train and told him, he confirmed it. After checking the station, I told him the arrival time of 4 am. I was holding my mother's hand from one hand and the mobile in the other.

Whatever my mother said that night, people were thinking it to be a liver disease complication, called

Hepatic Encephalopathy. (Hepatic encephalopathy (HE) is an altered level of consciousness as a result of liver failure. The underlying mechanism is believed to involve the buildup of ammonia in the blood, a substance that is normally removed by the liver.) But everything she said, was scaring us because whatever she says often come true and at that time she was narrating the day (as Friday) and scene of her death. Somehow the morning came and we all tried to ask her about what was troubling her but she was not telling anything and was also not ready to eat anything. The nurse called the doctor on phone and informed him about her condition, "All her vitals are normal. I don't know why she is doing so. They would keep her in ICU unnecessarily."

The nurse correctly stated that the reason for her deteriorating condition was not related to hepatic encephalopathy or the liver. The nurse's insight saved a patient from going to the ICU.

After a lot of efforts by us, she told us that she was not able to see anything, she lost her vision and she was totally depressed that if she cannot see with her eyes then what will she do by remaining alive? This was very shocking for us. I have no words for her. What kind of a treatment was it that was taking her towards new diseases?

Everyone was shocked to hear this. Before the Doctor's round, his assistant came and checked her eyes, he placed the *pen's nib* near the patient's eyes. Suddenly, the nib of pen touched the eye ball and eye got closed, it looks like that the patient was just a material for an experiment. When the doctor came, he placed his finger near my mother's eyes to check her eyes but still his finger was far away from the eye ball. Then pointing towards me, he asked her, "Tell me, Who is this?" My mother said, "Say something." And when I did not said anything, she couldn't recognize me, then doctor asked, "How did you recognize me?" By voice... yes, she recognized the voice, that's why when he asked who I was, she told me to speak.

When someone told the doctor about what his assistant had done (checking her eye with the pen), he got angry at his assistant and scolded him for doing so.

Dr. Ahsan then gave reference to ophthalmologist and left. Next day, opthalmologist came and he introduced himself, unlike other doctors, whom we came to know by the time they were gone.

He asked about my mother's entire problem and explained to us the possible reasons of her condition and advised for fundoscopy test. Her test was done and then she came back. On asking about the report, we came to know that we will get the report by tomorrow, the nurse inquired but didn't get any report from there, neither on time nor later and not after discharge.

People very calmly consoled us by giving examples of some people that this happens due to side effects of medicines, it will get resolved itself in a day or two...don't worry, she will be better... And slowly in 2 days her vision became clear. How amazing these people are! they know everything...

Are they helpless before western treatment?

Are they cowards?

Or they are ignorant?

What kind of treatment is this? To focus on one disease so much that it will cause new problems so that the patient forgets about the first one. Is this the only purpose? Because Western (modern) medicine has found the cure for only a few diseases in 150 years. This question used to leave me perplexed and troubled every time.

The cleaning staff's wasteful expenditure beyond limits on everything in the name of the company's patients (referred cases), negligence in work, not giving doses in-time by the nursing staff and fooling the doctor by manipulating their own records, carelessness of the kitchen staff while preparing the patient's food (which on complaining they told me that it was happening because of overtime work), this was a new picture which was showing a different side of the reality of the doctor and the hospital. Which could not be seen from outside. Perhaps the destiny had brought us to the hospital to make us aware of this truth. While on one side the cleaning staff of government hospitals refused to work, on the other hand in private hospitals excessive wastage was happening in the name of cleaning after seeing the referred cases. On one side, the nursing staff was negligent in treatment of patients by wearing earplugs, in private hospital they were trying for central line to be placed so that they become free from changing the cannula repeatedly.

Among them all, there are some honest and responsible staff also.

Both right and wrong cannot be ignored. Disease goes aside, and patient remains entangled between right and wrong like *Tom and Jerry...*

CHAPTER 9

At the time of discharge, Dr. Ahsan sent her to Renal department as per the instructions of the nephrologist. She was taken to Dr. Rajeev, the senior urologist there, and Dr. Mohit. On seeing Dr. Ayush Tripathi's name, Dr. Rajeev closed the file and angrily told the nursing staff, "The patient was seen by Dr. Ayush, go and consult him, why have you brought her to me." This is a harsh reality of the medical profession where the patient sometimes gets injured and sometimes gets martyred in the silent war of doctors.

When the nursing staff took her to Dr. Ayush (Urologist) he again postponed it for 15-20 days. My mother requested Dr. Mohit for the test to be done as soon as possible so that we can go back home (Allahabad). Without listening to what she is saying, Dr. Mohit got angry at the patient, "Do you people want to stay here? Now go back home"...I had seen this behaviour of Dr. Mohit many times but now such behaviour with a sick patient, filled me with a quite fury. I held back my anger, though, and tried to respond calmly, "First listen to what she is saying, she too is worried about going home." It seemed as if Dr. Mohit had sworn that he would not let her treatment be completed. He wrote about changing the catheter and when my mother expressed concerns about the risks of infection caused by long-term indwelling catheters, he interrupted "Who told you that a catheter causes infection, it doesn't cause any infection." After listening to her, in anger he prescribed an antibiotic injection at the time of changing the catheter.

- If it doesn't cause infection then why did he prescribed the antibiotic injection??

In this way she was discharged from there on 15th October 2019 without getting the treatment which was needed.

Coming out of the hospital gate we prayed that we will never have to see the face of any hospital again.

New city, new place but still we were trying our best to arrange all the things that she needed, no body made us feel that we were far away from home… yet no one can find the comfort of their own home outside. Now we were just waiting for the tests to be done, consult the doctor and go back to our city.

Again we took the reports and after persistent effort we have got an appointment with another urologist, Dr. Abhijeet for the test after a week. Now there was no other option except staying there for a week. The appointment was of 24th October at 12 pm. We reached there on time. Met the doctor, he told us that he is going for surgery and will conduct the test after coming back. So we have to wait for two more hours. After quite a while the doctor came. The test was started without any preparation, under the supervision of the nursing staff.

We were sitting in the waiting area and praying. Finally, the root cause of her illness will be known and her treatment will become easy.

I don't know for how many years we were waiting for the prayers to be answered...

I was praying in my mind when suddenly someone interrupted by asking a question "How did you came here?" No one else but Dr. Mohit was standing in front of us. My father said that we had an appointment for the test. After hearing this Dr. Mohit went straight from there to the doctor's cabin. And after ten minutes, Dr. Abhijeet called us and started getting angry "Why are you all insisting on getting the test done? The patient is so weak, admit her first and then get the test done."

This was the same person who was talking to us very nicely some time back. When she was admitted, they told us to get the test done after discharge and now they are saying to admit her for the test. We were caught between conflicting advice.

I complained about this to the doctors but their silence was proving correct, the statement "A doctor never stands against another doctor."

When I asked my mother, she said with tears in her eyes "Why is he interfering with my treatment, why is he not letting me get treated?" On asking further, she told that Dr. Mohit had stopped the urologist from doing the test. After waiting for such a long time for the test, and then stopping the test in the middle, due to stress and fatigue, her condition deteriorated again, and we found ourselves back at the hospital the next day to get her admitted.

It was *Dhanteras*, there was no cab or auto available during the night, so after a lot of efforts somehow we managed to admit her to the hospital. Most of the patients had already been discharged from the hospital due to the festival. On the day of *Diwali,* she had a little stomach ache since morning, so the nurse told us to inform the doctor when he comes for his rounds. We were waiting for the doctor's round. Even after several hours when none of the two doctors came for their rounds, we asked the nurse and she said, "It is *Diwali* today, he may not come, he must be celebrating Diwali."

What will happen to the patients if the doctor who takes a five minutes round in 24 hours does not come even for five minutes??

Nowadays, where hospitals have become healthcare companies and doctors their employees, is it easy for them to take leave??

May be they get stuck in their own problems! Does anyone even think about this??

Dr. Mehra came for rounds in the evening, his face was red with cold and fever, it was a festival, still he came for rounds. Was this an employee's compulsion or the doctor's duty?? Whatever it may be, he took the prayers of a patient and left.

After 2-3 days my mother was discharged and we took her to OPD for follow up three days later as per doctor's instructions. Dr. Ahsan was writing the name on the prescription when he received someone's call. As soon as he received the call, someone from the other side was continuously complaining that he had not come to see a patient. He tried to make them understand for quite some time and finally told them that his own daughter was admitted in the hospital. He could not be able to visit due to her hospitalization. This was the reason why the doctor not came to the hospital on *Diwali*. Are doctors not human beings? Do they or anyone in their family not get sick?? This incident of Dr. Mehra and Dr. Ahsan has proved that nothing is one-sided, doctors are also a part of society, everyone will have to face the evils committed by society regarding treatment, even if they are doctors.

- ✦ Are these incidents showing a different sides of the healthcare system??
- ✦ Whether these are challenges of the medical field?? Or medical errors??

CHAPTER 10

Due to negligence during the tests, her liver disease progressed suddenly. Gastro doctors were repeatedly insisting for kidney treatment.

Everything has some pros and cons, similarly everyone knows the advantages of specialization in the medical field. Doctor being expert in a particular field, will do the correct treatment. But have you ever thought about the negative side?? In the world of medical specialization—where the body is divided into neat, manageable sections, and specialists focus so intensely on their corner of the human puzzle that they often fail to see the bigger picture. While saving one organ, often other organs get damaged. They focus so much on a particular organ that hundreds of new diseases get discovered but the discovery of how the treatment will be done is going on for centuries. Treatment is based only on the concept of cuts (surgery/amputation), removal (removal, eg. tooth/gallbladder stone etc.), replacement/transplantation. Here also both the Liver specialists knew the treatment. Despite being Gastro specialists, those doctors first fulfilled the duty of being doctors and treated the case as far as it was possible for them. But they were unable to take the treatment further because their humanity was trapped under their specialization.

This time when she was discharged, we wanted to take her back home (Allahabad) but the doctors advised us to stay for 4-5 days and told us to immediately consult a kidney doctor.

By the time she was discharged, it was evening and the time to meet the kidney doctor at the hospital was over. After this, we went to his residential clinic, whose exact location or timing we didn't knew and I had no idea how to reach there.

Every step of this journey felt like a maze I had to solve in real time. I somehow managed to find out the doctor's contact number and then taken the number for consultation. From there I found out the timing and found the address from Google maps and reached his clinic. I showed the reports to the doctor and told him everything. He prescribed medicines for a month and he had marked *COLISTIN* in the culture report with a pen and said "Tell the concerned doctors not to prescribe this antibiotic *'Colistin'* as it will cause kidney failure, because her kidneys are already severely compromised." Taking care of what a senior nephrologist said also got added to my responsibilities.

Five days later, after follow up, we returned back home (Allahabad). We came back home at night, it was 11:30 and as soon as I reached home, I fed her a small piece of sweet (dessert) and hugged her tightly. I wished her a happy birthday, the tears I had held back for so long began to flow. It was her birthday, November 9th. I said, "This time I want a gift from you, please get well soon, I just want to see you healthy again."

I also promised myself that from tomorrow my efforts will have a new beginning and my efforts will go to the extent of making possible the circumstances that seems to be impossible.

In the morning, I again gathered my scattered courage and started trying.

These efforts included every treatment that heals the mind, body and soul. It is said that if efforts are made with a true heart, success is certain. After working hard day and night for 15-20 days, I got a good response.

Her good reports boosted my morale but I got real happiness on the day when I held her hand as usual to go from one place to another and she jolted my hand saying "Let me walk myself." As soon as she jolted my hand I started to stumble and my mother herself caught me. My mother was regaining her strength. This was such a precious moment for me that I felt happy even after getting the jolt. Every time I used to hold her hand with the hope that she would not need my support. Because if a person who remains active all the time suddenly needs someone's help, their courage breaks.

Again it felt like life is slowly coming on track, efforts were succeeding. In the darkness of sadness a flame of hope had been lit. My mother decided to remove the catheter now. But I stopped her by saying, "Let me try just one more time, after that I will not stop you, you will remove it yourself." By saying this, may be I extinguished that flame of hope with my own hands.

One month got completed and it was time for follow up. The plan was to first consult to a kidney doctor, and then try for UDS in the meantime and it's good if they will do the test and remove catheter otherwise we will go to the gastro doctor and come back and as she said, I will not stop her from removing the catheter. Plan!!! Life doesn't follow our plans, life has it's own way called DESTINY.

On 29th November, we left the house after meeting everyone. My grandfather gave his blessings to her to come back safely. The journey had just started when she started feeling nauseous, which was a common thing for us while travelling by road. She vomited but there was blood in it (which is called *Hematemesis* in medical terminology) seeing this we were shocked. We could not understand anything, we got down from the car, now we were in the city, the hospital was nearby at a distance of two minutes and on the other side it was a long journey of 200 kilometers. The driver left the car and went away, we were standing in the middle of the road and could not understand anything. My mother said "I don't want to go to new hospital and new doctor again. Take me there, I will live further if my life is written in my destiny."

The fear of starting a new treatment gave her courage to undertake a 200 kilometer long journey even when she is suffering from Hematemesis or was this the same fear which she had experienced 25 years back... due to not being able to reach the far away hospital in emergency, she had to undergo treatment at a nearby hospital which ruined her life.

My uncle decided to continue the journey on my mother's insistence. Will we be able to reach there or not?? It did not seem possible to take her there safely, so the driver also started refusing to go, saying, what if something happened on the way??

On our insistence, the driver moved the car forward. But throughout the way he kept saying, "These people have gone mad, something will happen to her on the way." I called the doctor and told him about my mother's condition, first he Advised us to buy an injection from a nearby pharmacy to control the bleeding, but then he refused. He asked about a hospital nearby. I told him that she is not willing to go back to Allahabad (some new hospital). Then the doctor said, "Then continue your journey by having faith in God."

It was suspected that the EVL banding had ruptured. The treatment must be going to start with endoscopy again.

Hearing about continuing the journey, my uncle was continuously getting calls. Everyone was telling him not to go ahead, don't take such a major risk, if something happens, everyone would blame you for committing a blunder mistake.

For the one who has taken the entire home responsibility upon herself, sacrified her job, her talent, her happiness, her dreams for the sake of their happiness, how easily these people suggested him not to take responsibility of her. Nowadays when people are afraid of taking responsibility for their own people, what should a person expect from others?

- Will those words of the driver that frightened us be true?
- Or the quote that says "Never Give Up" in difficult and impossible situations?

CHAPTER 11

The journey continued, a journey which neither had any assurance of completion nor was there any idea of the destination. We were moving ahead with the faith in God only.

The view of sunset, the soft light of the evening, the setting sun and the darkness of the night were so scary for the first time in my life. There were just a few hours which seemed like centuries. We reached the city but got stucked in traffic jam on the city's outer side and the closed railway crossing took an hour.

Reaching the hospital gate was not less than a miracle for us. My mother was admitted in emergency. This journey and her condition had broken my courage. Now I couldn't be able to hold my tears even in front of my mother and I had no words to console her either. Our struggle to reach the hospital after a long journey of 200 km was successful, now it was the turn of the doctors.

The emergency duty doctor called Dr. Ahsan and informed him about the arrival of the patient, Dr. Ahsan told him about the treatment and advised to arrange two units of blood.

In that situation my mother prayed that she would not need blood transfusion again. Not just because of the fear of allergic reaction that she had suffered last time but because she did not want anyone to donate blood to her. How can asking for blood be acceptable to a person who has always tried not to be the cause of anyone's suffering.

Her prayers were answered by the Almighty. In the morning when Dr. Ahsan came for rounds, after seeing the blood reports he could not believe that a patient who had vomited blood still her *haemoglobin* came out to be 14 in the report. He scolded the nurse "This report is not correct, get the test done again." During this entire treatment, 1-2 units of blood were taken out just in the name of sample for testing.

She was not ready at all for endoscopy again. As I was already scolded by her, when I tried to convince her for endoscopy, so I told the doctor that she is not ready for endoscopy. But the doctor strictly told her that endoscopy is necessary, it would be done at 3 pm and after informing the nurse for endoscopy he went away from there.

When I tried to convince her for endoscopy, she reminded me about the clamp injury during the previous endoscopy.

On hearing this, we asked the nurse where we can find the doctor now? The nurse told us that he would be in the OPD. We went there and reminded him about the clamp injury and requested him to take care of it at this time. He assured us that it would not be repeated again.

We were waiting outside for the endoscopy when a lady who had came for her husband's treatment saw us in distress and asked me about my mother and us. Then she read something and prayed for my mother, she put her hand on my head and prayed for her speedy recovery. There was no relation, we were complete strangers. I felt the power of humanity at that moment.

This time she didn't felt pain like before and she came back after 5-10 minutes from endoscopy room. And after 2-3 hours, she was allowed to eat but could not be able to eat it because of pain.

Today, in the name of *'Advanced Technology'*, we are only diverting our mind from our pain and suffering. *'Scopes'* have increased the scope a lot. When something is used excessively, it becomes the cause of disaster.

Next morning when Dr. Mehra came, on asking about the report he told us "It was an ulcer which had bled, medicines will be given, it will slowly get healed, there is nothing to worry about, this is a side effect of *EVL banding*, this often happens after EVL."

Once a person gets entangled in treatment, he does not even realize when he has moved from treatment of diseases to treatment of side effects.

In the evening, when Dr. Ahsan came on his rounds, the nurse showed him the blood report. Haemoglobin was 12. "There is no need to arrange blood." On hearing this, my mother thanked God that she did not needed blood.

Dr. Ahsan was still confused by the report that came after repeating the test. "How the haemoglobin is maintained even after so much bleeding?" It seemed as if he had asked the question to himself.

But I was neither surprised nor had any confusion because this time which I spent at home in taking care of her rather than wasting it in saving her from the mistakes made by fifty type of staffs in hospital. I had faith not just in my own care but also in the treatment of two experts (doctors). The weekly injections of *Zyrop (erythropoietin)* prescribed by a senior nephrologist were also having an effect. If the right medicine and good care will be given on time then it leads to speedy recovery of patient.

Am I trusting the doctors and treatment?

Well..! I always trusted them because my mother always made me aware about the work at every level in the hospital and its treatment, the struggle of the patients, both the responsible and careless behaviour of the hospital staff, the life of the doctors and the challenges that comes in the healthcare system. And now this experience of observing so deeply the Physician's burnout, their frustration, ego clashes, silent war among them and deception. I came to see the healthcare system from a different perspective.

One thing in the world that is considered as most breakable is trust. But the speciality of this trust/belief is that it never breaks. Trust either exists or it does not exist. Every human being has both positives and negatives just like every coin has two sides. *'Trust'* is the name of this complete belief. That's why we don't mark its arrival, for it slips in as naturally as breath.

The person who keeps the good aspects dominant appears trustworthy and the one who keeps the bad aspects dominant is considered as a deceiver. Trust is an earning which is not earned by just saying it. But it is earned only when a person fulfills his responsibilities and duties with discipline, sticks to his word, speaks the truth, has the courage to accept his mistake when needed. We don't realize we've entrusted someone until the moment of betrayal (until the other side of coin get revealed). We swore never to trust again, but we had already done so without thinking, without knowing. But where both honesty and corruption are present, it is foolish to trust anyone.

CHAPTER 12

If our belief is strong and efforts are true, then every success is possible. After 3-4 days, getting discharged from the hospital on her own feet was proving this to be true.

Then what went wrong??

Because the efforts were incomplete, leaving aside the treatment that was needed, all other unnecessary treatments were being done. This was the reason for her repeated hospitalization.

If the patient gets cured after getting the right treatment, then why would anyone come to the hospital?? This question often arises... Is it true?

If any doctor sets out with the thought that he will cure all the patients, his life will reach the end but the diseases will not end. Diseases will keep on coming as long as the world exists. Similarly, greed also never ends. It is just a matter of a our intentions that makes a difference, what we like, which path we choose!

This time when we went for follow-up, she just walked holding my hand without any help. My father said to Dr. Ahsan, "Today she didn't need any support, she came here on her own." A doctor can get success with money but gets satisfaction only when his patient comes on their feet from the stretcher or wheelchair. In today's world, where medicine has increasingly become a business, such moments are rare and precious as not every doctor is lucky enough to have this blessing. Everyone is giving priority to money over satisfaction.

I gave him my mother's reports, he was surprised and asked her "Whose report is this? Whether he had taken the sample of your blood or did he collected someone else's sample?" And then he seriously told my mother, "I haven't seen such a good reports of Liver Cirrhosis patient, your report is very good."

My eyes were filled with tears of joy. I was longing to hear something good.

"There was only one problem, kidney infection and catheter." When Dr. Ahsan warned me about the kidney problem again, this time I said, "We have tried a lot but neither they are doing the test nor they are allowing us to remove catheter. We don't know any other doctor in this city. Suggest someone whom you think is best." Then, Dr. Ahsan referred Dr. Suresh on prescription, who was another nephrologist of the same hospital.

We got an appointment with Dr. Suresh after three days but a night before his appointment her health deteriorated again. Seeing her moving towards unconscious condition everyone was shocked. It was a cold December night, at 2:30 am, I checked her blood glucose level which was normal. I told my father to get BP monitor from aunt. Somehow, he managed to get the digital sphagmomanometer, so I checked her BP. Seeing 80/32 we did not believed it, so I checked my uncle's BP whose BP used to be high. His BP was high then aunt's was also normal. Now my condition was the same which used to happen when her blood glucose level fallen to 30. What should I do?? How to handle it?? I put salt on her tongue. Then my father reminded me of half boiled eggs and coffee. Somehow I fed it to her. In the meantime, from repeated calls from my family members, I was getting the same advice "Take her to the hospital." And by the time I could understand anything, my cousin called from Lucknow and sent an ambulance from the hospital.

Now I didn't have any option but to take her to hospital.

Seeing an ambulance itself creates a situation of panic. When we reached the hospital, all the things were monitored in the emergency, BP was now almost normal, everything else was also normal, so he said let the doctor come, he will tell us what to do. My mother's condition improved gradually. We were waiting for the doctor to come. A nurse came in emergency and asked about the blood reports of a patient whose surgery was planned for that day. The doctor called the nurse whose duty it was, she told him that her duty was over, so she took the sample and informed the next duty staff to send it away and left. They called the one who was on duty at that time. When the other nurse was called, she said I don't know. No one knows where the sample went. Then a nurse saw it and found that the sample was there in the fridge. Blood test was necessary so the doctor told them to send the fresh sample again for testing. And the surgery of that patient was postponed for the next day. If there is more staff then the blame game becomes easy. Well! Whoever is at fault doesn't matter, the patient has to bear the punishment.

When the doctor came and saw everything normal, he thought that we got panicked and took her to the hospital. How could I tell him that in the condition that we had seen, anyone else would have done the same. I told him that her BP was very low. I had just given her salt, half boiled egg and coffee. Listening to which Dr. Ahsan said "May be the BP monitor was not working properly, if such low BP was cured with egg and coffee then the ICU would not have been opened."

Such a low BP can be cured with egg and coffee, I would not have believed it if I had not gone through it myself. Many years ago, I had fainted due to very low blood pressure. Then my uncle (our family doctor) told my parents to give her half boiled egg and coffee immediately, due to which my BP got controlled in some time and I was saved from being rushed to hospital in an emergency. Since then I have always seen the positive results of this home remedy. I do not know what is the connection between this home remedy and ICU? Is it true or not? But I know one thing for sure that it's all about the lack of complete faith of human being. Because it is the faith that heals. Be it half boiled egg and coffee or ICU, it is the invention/discovery of faith.

After consulting the doctor, we came back with my mother as her condition became stable. Next day we had an appointment of Dr. Suresh for kidney treatment. We were waiting for the doctor to come, when suddenly she was feeling nauseous, someone made her sit on a wheelchair. Dr. Suresh seen her and we came outside and stood with her in the same waiting area. I was booking a cab and my uncle and father were getting medicine from the pharmacy. When Dr. Suresh passed from there, he saw my mother and said that "Don't take her home, she is not looking well, if her condition worsen at night it will create problem for her." We told him that this has happened many times. The gastro doctor had given medicine, she will be alright. He then saw some reports from earlier and took it from us and said, "I'm going to discuss the case with Dr. Ahsan and will then decide what to do." And he went to Dr. Ahsan's chamber.

After 5-10 minutes someone came and asked, "Are you with the patient? Doctor is calling you." When I went there, Dr. Ahsan said that her condition is getting worse due to kidney problems, there are some medicines which we cannot give, he is a nephrologist, he will treat her accordingly.

Dr. Suresh said, "Admit her just for 1 or 2 days, the vomiting problem will also be resolved and she will be discharged after getting the tests done." I told him that I do not want to admit her now and in Renal department, not at all. Dr. Suresh suggested us to admit her in any one of the two branch of hospital, if she gets admitted in Gastro unit then I will come whenever needed, and if she stays in Renal department then Dr. Ahsan will come. I said that I do not want to admit her anywhere now. On which Dr. Ahsan said "As she needs kidney treatment so it will be better to admit her in Renal department, test will also be done easily and if needed I will come there." I didn't said anything, we were trying for this 1-2 day treatment for the last 2 months and now the doctor himself was asking me to get it done, still my mind was not ready to admit her. May be I had lost faith in the treatment. Seeing my silence Dr. Ahsan reassured me "Don't worry, I will come there whenever needed".

Then my uncle went to get the referral papers, and we took her to the hospital. I'm getting the calls asking "Where are you?" On telling, everyone got worried as to what happened to her suddenly? Then I told them that she is okay, we admitted her for the tests, she will be discharged in 1-2 days after the tests. And in this way, we came to the OPD and reached the hospital.

- Was this just another example of the medical field being turned into a business?
- Or was it something more—a doctor's genuine concern for his patient, offering the care she truly needed?

CHAPTER 13

This was the last part of my mother's treatment. We were there in the hospital waiting to get her admitted when a lady arrived in the emergency ward, who was asking her family, why they had brought her here? Her son and daughter (both doctors) told her that few things in her reports are not normal so they were admitting her for treatment. When she insisted her daughter to take her back to home, her daughter reassured her "The doctor will discharge you in a day or two."

It was already late night, they shifted my mother to the room and the nurse took her sample for testing. In the morning, Dr. Suresh made his rounds. He talked about giving *"Colistin"* saying that "According to the culture report only this antibiotic is effective and there is no other option." The same antibiotic which the senior nephrologist had warned against, he marked in the culture report and said that if this antibiotic is given then it will cause kidney failure in her case. I informed Dr. Suresh about the senior nephrologist's warning and also requested him to discuss it with the senior nephrologist but he denied.

Their conflicts had escalated to a point where mistakes were made due to poor communication or collaboration and their fractured team failed to recognize errors, leading to negligence or subpar patient outcomes every time.

So, I told him clearly "If you are giving it, then give it on your responsibility, "Nothing should happen to my mother." Despite our refusal, he prescribed *'Colistin'* and left.

My heart still didn't agreed on his decision of prescribing Colistin, so I took my father to the OPD thinking that may be he would explain to him in a better way. But he had not changed his decision.

It was not known at what time the urologist would come and I had to go out for some important work. Meanwhile, the urologist (Dr. Rajeev) came in the evening, the same doctor who had sent the patient back last time saying, "The staff does not even give complete information, they haven't informed me that the patient is on a catheter." Now he was shifting the blame to others. Upon seeing the catheter, he angrily said, "Why has this catheter been inserted? Don't you know that catheter causes infection?"

"I know it causes infection, that's why I've been asking for it to be removed since two months," my mother replied. Then he checked the patient's record and after giving appointment for the next day, he left.

When I returned, I came to know that the doctor had already visited and said that he will conduct the test tomorrow. As her condition was stable and she doesn't need hospitalization, Dr. Suresh told us during the round that the test will be done tomorrow, so after keeping her under observation for a few hours, he will discharge her tomorrow itself. He also said that he has stopped *'Colistin'*, as she doesn't need this medication.

This was our last attempt because my mother had already decided that if the doctor will not do the test then she will remove the catheter herself and this time I will support her in her decision.

The happiness of a few moments vanished, as usual. In a short while she reached the ICU. Her Blood Pressure (BP) gradually fell, and she was shifted to the ICU.

They administered *Noradrenaline (Norad)* to stabilize her BP, and for that, inserted a central line into her neck. Eventually I lost this battle also. *Central line* was inserted after making an incision in the neck. On going to the ICU, my mother told me about the pain that she had gone through. I was so talkative especially with my mother that my conversations with her would not end until my mother would say that even the radio goes off at 12 am, now try to sleep. But now, I have no words even to console her. The pain which she had felt for some time will going to hurt me for the rest of my life.

I came out and sat on the granite placed on the large glass window built on the stairs. It was the cold night of December, the rainwater flowing through the glass of the window, the granite was so cold that it felt like we were sitting on snow. The staff came there and told us to vacate the room as your patient is shifted to ICU. My father went to the reception and requested them to give us some time as it was mid night and raining but they denied and their conversation started turning into a heated discussion. The staff was compelled by their duty, their humanity was breaking down before the rules of the hospital. As soon as I felt this, I told my father to understand that these rules were not made by them, "They are just doing their duty. Why are you arguing with them, look at the helplessness of the staff." I had put my patience over my helplessness and I assured them that I'm going to vacate the room. I took my father from there to take out the stuff from the room. I was taking out the stuff when the same person who had just asked me to vacate the room came and gave us time till his duty hours. Perhaps my words had shaken humanity.

By not taking advantage of anyone's help, we vacated the room an hour before his given time. Somehow the night was spent outside the ICU, on the stairs and in the room.

In the morning, Dr. Suresh said that the kidney treatment should be done as per the opinion of the liver doctor and said that a reference has been given to the gastro doctor, after getting his opinion the treatment will be done accordingly. I kept on waiting at the hospital gate throughout the day. As Dr. Ahsan had paid attention to what the senior nephrologist said, therefore, it was hoped that he would understand the mistake in treatment and he would explain it to the doctor and help in the right treatment.

At 10 o'clock at night the watchman standing at the gate asked "You are standing here since morning, for whom you are waiting?" I said about the doctor. He replied

"Doctor's visiting hours are over, it is already 10 o'clock, it's very cold and raining, go inside." Next day also, we got the same reply from Dr. Suresh on his rounds and we kept waiting. On the third day when he again said the same thing, so I told him to get her kidney treated first and for liver treatment, "Dr. Mehra also knows about my mother's case. Why are you all not calling him? If Dr. Ahsan is not coming, then give reference to Dr. Mehra, why are you delaying the treatment?" To this, he said that the hospital is nearby, you should go and tell him to come.

A person can sense most of the lies, deceptions and mistakes before it actually happens but people's stubbornness in dismissing the facts by creating fear and demanding proof makes the person lose. I was tired now, not with my mother's treatment, but with people's lies and deceptions.

My uncle took us there. A huge crowd of patients was waiting outside the cabin. On asking, we came to know that Dr. Ahsan is on IPD rounds. My uncle took us towards the stairs because doctors usually came from there. When Dr. Ahsan returned from rounds after some time, he saw us waiting near the stairs and came straight there and said, "I'm coming there, actually there was an emergency in my family and I was busy to get them hospitalized, then due to the patients there and here, I could not come."

His reaction when he saw us there, was telling that he didn't forget about the reference but could not find time... Why?

May be because of the pressure that doctors have on them, sometimes to build their and their family's status in the society and sometimes to save their job in the hospital, they need more patients and money. But in the midst of all this, they forgets that they also had only 24 hours in a day which cannot be extended to 25 hours.

What kind of complaint and what request can I make to someone who is not getting time even for himself and his family. I haven't said a single word. Dr. Ahsan said again, "I'm coming there after seeing the patients."

In the evening, when Dr. Ahsan came, we were called in the ICU. I went there with my father. Dr. Hetal and Dr. Mohit were standing with Dr. Ahsan.

- ✦ What were two duty incharges doing in ICU at the same time?? Whether it was a change of their shifts or something fishy?

Dr. Ahsan saw my mother and suggested to stop *'Colistin'* and get the *UDS* done and remove the catheter as soon as possible but Dr. Mohit refused it by saying that the patient's condition is not good, UDS cannot be done in such condition. Dr. Ahsan then said that *Colistin* is damaging the kidneys, on which Dr. Mohit laughed and replied that first, we will have to save the life, we will save the kidneys later on. (Although he was fully aware of the fact that her life was in danger due to the condition of her kidneys). Dr. Ahsan's argument went waste.

When Dr. Ahsan was about to leave, my father asked about the condition of her liver. He told him that if there will be *Ascities* it will be removed by *tapping* but her main problem is of kidneys. After saying this to my father, he tried to make me understand that these doctors are trying their best. But one day, everyone has to go. That girl, who used to fight even for small things for her mother was shouting from inside, 'What efforts are you talking about? And to whom are you trying to console, to me or to yourself? And I also know that everyone will have to go one day but who has given the right to you or your hospital to decide that one day??' But now, I didn't have the strength to even utter a word. I stood silently and Dr. Ahsan (along with the hope that he will come timely and will save my mother's life by stopping the wrong treatment) left from there. Yes! The same Dr. Ahsan who had assured us that he would come there whenever needed when I was not ready to admit her again.

I wonder what they had discussed with a cup of coffee when they suggested us to admit her just for one or two day for the test. Either they had decided to experiment on my mother with a *nephrotoxic antibiotic* or one doctor (Colleague) had betrayed the other?? The question that remained unanswered...

- Who got betrayed—the patient...(by their doctors) or a doctor (by his colleague) ??

CHAPTER 14

When Dr. Suresh was on his rounds, I asked him to shift her to the room (because they were probably just waiting for the patient's death). Dr. Suresh refused saying that she cannot be shifted in room as it's not possible to even shift her bed from here.

I requested them to please give the reference to Dr. Abhay (senior nephrologist), when he came, he told me that he had seen it. I tried to tell him but Dr. Mohit interrupted before I could finish my sentence. I tried again then Dr. Abhay said that Dr. Mohit had told me everything.

- ✦ Was this a doctor's blind trust in his assistant, or an attempt by a department director to save the doctors of his hospital??

Next day Dr. Suresh told me on his rounds that she would have to undergo *Dialysis*. On hearing this, I stumbled and was about to fall, a nurse quickly steadied me and helped me sit down. Shock took over—this was the nightmare I had feared, the cruel consequence of misguided treatment.

The patient's kidneys failed due to wrong treatment. To save her life, dialysis was needed. I was asked to sign the consent paper (permission letter). On one side, it was my mother's life and on the other, the promise that she had taken from me. When I tried to pick up the pen to sign, I remembered my mother's words that she said while taking me to the dead body of my aunt on which there were cuts in many places in the name of dialysis, fistula, central line and food pipe and had taken a promise from me that to save my life, never put me in such a situation, never prove your love with me this way. Your faith must be greater than your love. If God has written my life then no one take it otherwise no one can save me.

While thinking about it, I felt as if I was standing on a path where there was a well ahead and a valley behind. I tried to pick up the pen which felt like a knife that would hurt her and her trust in the name of dialysis and my hand moving towards the pen stopped. But this is a hospital, which gives you pain with your permission. It is guaranteed that you will get pain by going here but there is no guarantee that you will get relief from that pain, whether you will return home or not.

They took permission from another family member. Maybe I was saved from breaking the promise made to my mother but my desires, dreams and efforts related to her gets broken. We slowly and steadily keep torturing ourselves and sometimes our loved ones in the name of treatment and knowingly or unknowingly becomes a part of some research. You don't know where life will take you.

When I went from the waiting area towards the ICU, I saw that both the doctors (whose mother was admitted at the same time as my mother) were sitting and crying. On asking, it was revealed that their mother has been put on a ventilator.

At night, we were sitting in the waiting area when suddenly we heard a girl screaming loudly. I was not able to hear her screams. I sat down and put my hands on my ears. Screams will not end by keeping hands on the ears, truth will not change by closing eyes. I gathered my courage and got up, went towards the stretcher where that 14 years old girl was lying. Her old grandmother was crying nearby. When I went and asked, her old grandmother explained that due to their financial constraints, they had been forced to stop the girl's dialysis halfway. She was screaming in pain and discomfort and it felt as if there were corpses roaming around, or these people were used to seeing such cases.

I had the last 500 rupee note left in my purse. She was in need of 2500 rupees. I needs prayers and she needs money. I gave her that last 500 rupee note. My uncle came forward as soon as he saw me. On seeing us, the people nearby who were watching this scene for quite some time but were sitting silently, they also started giving and even the security guard there also contributed. In this way, we all helped her in arranging money and that girl's dialysis started again. Suddenly, her grandmother bent down to touch my feet, I was shocked and stepped back, saying, "Please don't do this, you are older than me." I lifted up her. She hugged me, and after giving me her blessings, she went towards the ICU with the girl.

For the past two days, two unsuccessful attempts at dialysis were made, but due to low BP, dialysis could not be done. After hearing this, my cousin arrived from Lucknow (who is a doctor and has also experienced his mother's kidney failure and dialysis), met with the doctors and found out that there was no facility for CRRT (dialysis done in low BP). On coming to know about this, he talked about shifting my mother to a higher institution where this facility was available. We decided to take her to Delhi next morning. On the other hand, the lady whose husband was continuously undergoing dialysis, and her family was now shifting their patient to Delhi.

At 6 pm (patient's meeting time) in the ICU, I along with my cousin went there but the guard stopped us. We heard the patient's screaming, which was coming from inside. I recognized the voice. I moved forward. The guard stopped us and said, "She is not your mother, there is another patient." But I recognized the screams coming continuously. I did not listen to him and moved forward then they closed the ICU door from inside. The guard threw us out from there. I came down to the waiting room and started crying, then my cousin took me to the ICU. It was time to meet the patient. When I went near my mother and asked the reason for the screaming, she pointed her finger towards a lady who was cleaning the floor and told us that her skin got rubbed due to pulling the bedsheet to change it. She said, "If I had been told, I would have changed sides on my own." While telling this, tears were coming out of her eyes due to the pain.

On hearing this, she threw the mob on the ground and angrily complained to the doctor "Look, she is complaining to her daughter." What will a person do when her patient is in ICU? I told that woman that she is sick, be careful, she would have helped you in changing the bedsheet if you told her. But now I became afraid to leave her there alone. I was just coming out of ICU when I stopped after seeing the cardiologist.

Now they had silently called a cardiologist for the low BP as they had realized that these people are not alone and their carelessness has became apparent and we were shifting her somewhere else. We would not have known if I had not recognized him while coming out of the ICU. I also don't know how I recognized him? Because I never met him before. The cardiologist told us that her heart is absolutely fine. The *hypotension* was because of kidneys and advised them to reduce the dosage of *Norad.* He said that may be the patient's BP remain on the lower side normally. Try reducing the dosage for some time or else will continue.

My cousin took me to meet Dr. Abhay (senior nephrologist) and she insisted to inform him about the whole situation, but here the same staff who had spoken very nicely to us earlier didn't allowed us to meet him when he came to know that my mother was now under the treatment of another nephrologist at the hospital.

They had already come to know that we were going to shift her to Delhi the next morning. When we went to the ICU for the doctor's round at night, we saw that my mother's bed had been shifted to the side. Now she too had realized the carelessness being shown to her, her whole face and eyes were swollen. She tried to say something but couldn't be able to speak, she just prayed for us and kept quiet.

A critical patient was just admitted on the bed next to my mother's bed. It was a delivery case, her condition was critical. Her husband folded his hands before the doctor and requested to save his wife. And the doctor said the same words that my mother's doctor had told my father about her critical condition 25 years ago. There was a similar scene in front of me, just like what my parents had gone through.

Now people are taking their loved ones to the hospital just to hear that there are some limitations of doctors and treatment too which they probably do not remember while taking money.

I came down and called my uncle and told him the whole situation. Now I did not have the strength to hear or understand anything else. I told him that they are treating my mother very negligently. He said "Don't worry, I'm coming we will take her in the morning." All that came out of my mouth was "Only if God takes her to the morning safely." Now he probably realized something and said, "Don't worry, we will shift her from there as soon as possible." I was sitting outside and crying in the rain and extreme cold of December. It felt as if the raindrops were supporting me in my grief.

Whatever we were afraid of, happened. At 6 a.m. in the morning they made an announcement that we were called to the ICU. I ran towards the ICU, the doctor told us that she was unable to breathe because fluid reached in her lungs, that is why we have put her on the ventilator.

I ran towards my mother and held her hand, the hand that always strongly held mine and gave me peace, today it slipped. When I saw the reading on the monitor, the dosage of *Norad* was low. Whatever the cardiologist had told them, they just ignored. All the readings had completely gone down. My heart sank.

It was the time of *Fajr,* and the person for whom my father was praying in the mosque was taking her last breaths. When my uncle saw me crying, he forcibly took me out of ICU. Relatives from that city also came there, everyone was trying to console me.

My father went to ICU at 11 a.m.; and when he came back I started asking them in a loud voice what happened, why isn't he saying anything, why is he crying? "Have patience, your mother is no more." This one sentence had ruined my whole life, my dreams, my desires, my efforts, my happiness, everything was shattered into pieces. I ran towards the lift, the guard stopped me, and my father took me from there. Everyone from the hospital guard to the staff and the patients had tears in their eyes, I don't know why?

That old uncle, who had become hopeless seeing the condition of his wife and I had encouraged him by giving my uncle's example, when he saw me he put his hand on my head and started crying and said, "My child, you encouraged me yesterday and now you are losing your patience. Have patience. May God give you the strength and courage." Saying this, he fell on the chair and put his hands on his forehead; it seemed as if he had lost all his courage. When the grandmother of that 14-year-old girl who was undergoing dialysis heard this news from somewhere she came to me and I don't know how many blessings she gave me, "My child you are a diamond, have faith in God." in her own language but being disappointed as I was in shock, she went away wiping her tears.

That day, my family had taken away a live-corpse from there along with the dead body of my mother. Suddenly, I stopped at the door and a voice came from inside that even if everything is known to you, will you go away like this? Neither I was in a condition of accepting the truth nor in a state to decide what I should have to do? As anger, hatred and helplessness crossed the limits, just one sentence came out from my mouth... *Innallaha-ma-as-sabireen...*

What a return gift they had given us—wrapped in white cloth.

CHAPTER 15

Where one story ends, a new story begins. But this was no ordinary beginning—this was the true start of a battle for survival. Life, with all its struggles, had just revealed its harshest truth to me. A person never dies alone, no one knows how many dreams and desires they take away with them, and leaves behind many living corpses, who, in the struggle to stay alive, lose their lives one day.

Truth had now closed all the ways for me to escape. There was only one way—to accept the truth and save others. I was not able to believe in the truth, and the one who could not be able to save her mother, how would she save others?

Court case..? Is it the only way??

No Way...! This was even beyond my thinking.

The screams of patients, their tears and helplessness of family members created a storm inside me which was not going to stop even if I tried to stop it. On top of that, you get free advice from people... Are you going to file court case? You are going to waste your life in running from pillar to post around the courts... You will get nothing except a lot of dates... There may be a few doctors who will misuse their power for succeeding the case... May be your own lawyer will keep you in the dark by shaking hands with the opposite party. My dear! you are nothing in front of reputed hospital... Try to understand that what happened was God's will. You can do nothing. etc.

Where does this thinking go while getting treatment? Even a mistake appears right at that time. People make the doctors sit on the throne, only to throw them on the floor. Are these people friends of the doctors or their enemies? I think this is the side effect of buying degrees with money. Everyone has seen the actions of hospitals during *Covid 19* where the urgency for medical supplies has led to corrupt procurement practices such as overpricing and favoritism. But still those who always ran after money could not even save their lives with their money. Did *Covid* not affected the doctors?

The actual enemies of doctors or any dedicated healthcare professionals are not those who files a case for addressing these issues but those silent killers of *'trust'*, working among them and the wrong mindset of society that from admission into medical college to admission in hospital they can buy anything with money. Everything seems right when it comes to secure the future of your child. The reason behind choosing this profession is just money nowadays, not the interest of that student. Parents, in their desperate desire for their children to succeed, had lost sight of what truly mattered. Their dream was no longer about nurturing a passion for healing—it was about securing a future of wealth and status. Every parents (either medical or non-medical professional) want their child to be a doctor no matter how (either by cheating or giving bribe/donations) but they are not ready to be treated by any such child of others. Our society is playing a crucial role in such issues. Doing harm would inevitably harm you in return, so ***'First, do no harm'*** because ***'Prophylaxis is better than cure'.***

I had gotten the answers of all my questions by now.

But there are still some questions left that can only be answered by time.

Will such a weak and fearful girl be able to go to court??

Yes, neither for the patients who are suffering not just from the disease but also from the pain of negligence, nor because there are some bad doctors due to whom not just the patients but every doctor is at risk, but for the woman for whom this fight is being fought. I didn't know if I could win this battle. But I did know this: I had learned the most important lesson from the woman I had loved most—the one whose absence left a void I couldn't fill. She had taught me to stand against evil, to trust that truth would always, in the end, find its way and she has made me experience that if the intentions are good, the paths will be created on it's own.

Truth always wins. Will my thought going to win or the words of people??

Now I also want the answer...

www.ingramcontent.com/pod-product-compliance
Lightning Source LLC
La Vergne TN
LVHW041121150826
845673LV00007B/2141

* 9 7 9 8 8 9 6 9 9 9 7 2 0 *